PREFACE

1. Scope

This publication provides joint doctrine for the planning and execution of US logistics in support of the Armed Forces of the United States during multinational operations.

2. Purpose

This publication has been prepared under the direction of the Chairman of the Joint Chiefs of Staff (CJCS). It sets forth joint doctrine to govern the activities and performance of the Armed Forces of the United States in joint operations and provides the doctrinal basis for US military coordination with other US Government departments and agencies during operations and for US military involvement in multinational operations. It provides military guidance for the exercise of authority by combatant commanders and other joint force commanders (JFCs) and prescribes joint doctrine for operations, education, and training. It provides military guidance for use by the Armed Forces in preparing their appropriate plans. It is not the intent of this publication to restrict the authority of the JFC from organizing the force and executing the mission in a manner the JFC deems most appropriate to ensure unity of effort in the accomplishment of the overall mission.

3. Application

a. Joint doctrine established in this publication applies to the Joint Staff, commanders of combatant commands, subunified commands, joint task forces, and subordinate components of these commands, and the Services.

b. The guidance in this publication is authoritative; as such, this doctrine will be followed except when, in the judgment of the commander, exceptional circumstances dictate otherwise. If conflicts arise between the contents of this publication and the contents of Service publications, this publication will take precedence unless the CJCS, normally in coordination with the other members of the Joint Chiefs of Staff, has provided more current and specific guidance. Commanders of forces operating as part of a multinational (alliance or coalition) military command should follow multinational doctrine and procedures ratified by the United States. For doctrine and procedures not ratified by the United States, commanders should evaluate and follow the multinational command's doctrine and procedures, where applicable and consistent with US law, regulations, and doctrine.

For the Chairman of the Joint Chiefs of Staff:

CURTIS M. SCAPARROTTI
Lieutenant General, U.S. Army
Director, Joint Staff

Intentionally Blank

SUMMARY OF CHANGES
REVISION OF JOINT PUBLICATION 4-08
DATED 25 SEPTEMBER 2002

- **Updates information on the joint logistics environment in multinational operations.**

- **Updates multinational logistics principles.**

- **Updates supply operations for logistics capabilities.**

- **Revises operational contract support and national security element to accurately reflect extant capabilities and processes.**

- **Deletes multinational logistics planning by operation phase.**

- **Adds predeployment planning to multinational logistics planning.**

- **Adds chapter for executing multinational logistics.**

- **Updates Appendix A (Commander's Checklist for Logistics in Support of Multinational Operations).**

- **Updates Appendix C (Relevant Legal Authorities for United States Logistics in Support of Multinational Operations).**

- **Revises and updates Appendix D (United States Contracting Considerations in Multinational Operations).**

- **Deletes Appendix E (Multinational Planning Augmentation Team).**

- **Deletes Appendix F (Logistics Security to Distribution Operations).**

- **Updates references and glossary.**

Intentionally Blank

TABLE OF CONTENTS

CHAPTER V
COMMAND AND CONTROL

APPENDIX

GLOSSARY

FIGURE

EXECUTIVE SUMMARY
COMMANDER'S OVERVIEW

- **Describes the Joint Logistics Environment in Multinational Operations**

- **Discusses Logistics Imperatives**

- **Explains Multinational Logistics Principles**

- **Discusses the Core Multinational Logistic Capabilities of Supply, Maintenance Operations, Deployment and Distribution, Health Service Support, Engineering, Logistic Services, and Operational Contract Support**

- **Provides Multinational Logistics Planning Guidance**

- **Addresses Command and Control of Multinational Logistics Operations**

Overview

Multinational logistics is any coordinated logistic activity involving two or more nations supporting a multinational force under the auspices of an alliance or coalition.

Logistic support during multinational operations differs from unilateral joint operations in that the participating nations represent different national and military objectives, cultures, and approaches to logistic support. This impacts how the US organizes, prepares, and executes logistic support during multinational operations. A significant challenge in multinational logistics (MNL) involves establishing effective command and control (C2) processes that are acceptable to all troop contributing nations.

The Joint Logistics Environment in Multinational Operations

The joint logistics environment exists at the strategic, operational, and tactical levels of war. Operations are distributed and conducted rapidly and simultaneously across multiple operational areas within a single theater or across boundaries of more than one geographic combatant commander and can involve a variety of military, interagency, nongovernmental organizations, commercial, and multinational partners.

Logistics Imperatives

The value of logistics can be determined by how well the force is deployed and sustained. Three logistic imperatives help determine this: unity of effort, joint logistics enterprise-wide visibility, and rapid and precise response.

Multinational Logistics

Because participating forces represent sovereign nations, there are several unique principles for MNL operations.

Principles	Although first formulated in North Atlantic Treaty Organization (NATO) documents, these principles are adaptable to all multinational operations. These principles are: collective responsibility, authority, primacy of operational requirements, cooperation, coordination, assured provision, sufficiency, efficiency, flexibility, visibility and transparency, synergy, simplicity, and timeliness.
Special Considerations	The planning and conduct of logistics in operations involving multiple sovereign nations characteristically differs from that in unilateral operations. Some of the special considerations include: the impact of national sovereignty, the US as a provider and recipient of logistic support, and differences in multinational logistics based on organizational structure, impact on MNL by type of operation, and force protection.

Logistics Capabilities

Core Multinational Capabilities	The core multinational logistic capabilities are: supply, maintenance operations, deployment and distribution, health service support (HSS), engineering, logistic services, and operational contract support. When combined with multinational personnel service support, they provide the ability to globally project and sustain the multinational force (MNF).
Supply Operations	Logisticians integrate the three functional capabilities of managing supplies and equipment, managing inventory, and managing supplier networks within the supply core logistic capability. Visibility of requirements and demands is critical for supplies and it requires communication and integration with other areas affecting the supply chain, maintenance, and distribution.
Maintenance Operations	Maintenance operations deliver systems readiness for the multinational force commander (MNFC). Each member nation executes maintenance as a core logistic capability to maintain the fleet readiness of units and capabilities.
Deployment and Distribution	The deployment and distribution capability supports the movement of forces and unit equipment during the deployment and redeployment processes, and supports materiel movement during the sustainment of operations.

Health Service Support	Nations are ultimately responsible for providing HSS for their forces. Because of national sensitivities, the US strives to rely on national resources for providing HSS to its forces to the maximum extent. The joint force surgeon is responsible for overall planning and coordination of medical support for the MNF.
Engineering	MNF engineers integrate, synchronize, and direct engineer operations. These functions include combat engineering, general engineering, and geospatial engineering.
Logistic Services	Nations participating in a multinational operation may determine the need for operational-level support organizations to provide common support for the MNF. Such organizations include naval advanced logistic support sites and naval forward logistic sites for supporting multinational maritime forces, and intermediate staging bases for supporting ground and air units.
Operational Contract Support	Centralized coordination of contracting efforts is essential to management of limited resources to ensure that the MNFC's operational priorities are effectively and efficiently supported. Through centralized coordination of contracting efforts, maximum benefits are derived from volume procurements, competition is optimized, price escalation is avoided, and the opportunities for local black market operations are minimized.
National Support Element	A national support element (NSE) is any national organization or activity that supports national forces that are part of an MNF. NSEs serve as the intermediary between the strategic level of logistic support from nations to their forces at the tactical level. They also coordinate and consolidate common-user logistics functions.
Host-Nation Support	**Host-nation support (HNS) will often be critical to the success of a multinational operation.** Centralized coordination of HNS planning and execution will ensure that limited HNS resources are allocated most effectively to support the MNFC's priorities. The more limited HNS resources are in the operational area, the greater the requirement for centralized management.
Funding and Reimbursement	In general, nations are expected to fund their participation in multinational logistic support arrangements and reimburse providers for any support received from other nations. Funding and reimbursement requirements for US

participation in these arrangements are generally a function of the applicable US legal authority.

Multinational Logistic Planning

Planning Guidance

Centralized coordinated planning is required to ensure smooth MNF deployment. The allocation of HNS and operational contract support reduces logistic footprints. Logistic planning of multinational operations poses considerable challenges. Realistically, only a few nations can logistically support themselves in every operational phase: deployment; sustainment; and redeployment/ termination.

Planning

When functioning as the MNFC, US commanders have the responsibility to develop a concept of operations and initial concept of support, in coordination with participating nations. US MNFC should address: logistic C2 relationships and organizational structure; structure, staffing, and equipment of MNL organizations; logistic authorities and responsibilities of the MNFC and participating nations; logistic reporting requirements and reporting capabilities of participating nations; and the interoperability of logistic C2, communications, and information systems within the force. In addressing these issues, US MNFC should keep in mind cultural aspects of multinational partners that could affect the operation (e.g., dietary preferences, physical characteristics, and religious practices and taboos).

Executing Multinational Logistics

Multinational Logistics Execution

Forces participating in multinational operations have two distinct chains of command: a national chain of command and a multinational chain of command. Adhering to the command authority that is negotiated between the participating nations during execution is essential in order to deconflict competition for limited resources, infrastructure, and to facilitate achieving unity of effort in MNF operations. Executing cooperative logistics in multinational operations is conducted using the lead nation (LN) method, pooled assets and resources method, or the role specialization agreement method.

Transitioning to a Multinational Operation

The US may find it necessary to initiate military action before an international consensus develops. Following the development of international support, a multinational operation, conducted by an alliance or a coalition, possibly under United Nations (UN) or NATO management, may be authorized. Since the US may have an extensive logistic structure already in place in the operational area, it may be asked to assume the lead role in the MNL organization—at least for a transition period. The US may also be asked to assume LN and role specialists nation roles.

Command and Control

General Guidance

The C2 structure for managing logistics during a multinational operation includes the authorities and responsibilities exercised by the MNFC and nations and the C2 through which the MNFC and nations exercise their assigned authorities and responsibilities. The logistic C2 structure established for a multinational operation should complement and be integral to the operation's overall C2 structure.

Authorities and Responsibilities

The four levels of command authority available to US commanders are: combatant command (command authority) (COCOM), operational control (OPCON), tactical control (TACON), and support. Other authorities outside the command relations include administrative control, coordinating authority, and direct liaison authorized. Each of these levels of authority—except COCOM—may apply to logistic forces assigned to a multinational operation.

Operational Control. In multinational operations, the US and other participating nations continue to exercise command over their forces throughout the operation. Generally, however, nations give the MNFC OPCON over their assigned forces (with qualifications discussed in Joint Publication (JP) 3-16, *Multinational Operations,* for placing US forces under OPCON of UN commanders). One element of OPCON, which is also shared by NATO, is that OPCON of itself does not include authority over administrative and logistic functions. Thus, in granting OPCON of US forces to the MNFC, the degree of MNFC coordination and tasking over administrative and logistic functions must be specified.

Tactical Control. The MNFC may be given authority to exercise TACON of ground units transiting through the joint security area. This consideration may apply regardless of whether the operational area resembles the traditional linear or nonlinear operational area.

Coordination Authority. Typically, the US and other nations will grant the MNFC coordinating authority over common logistic matters during a multinational operation. Under coordinating authority, the MNFC can require consultation between forces but does not have the authority to compel agreement. Coordinating authority recognizes the consultation relationship necessary for forces of sovereign nations to reach consensus during multinational operations to achieve the objective.

Other Authorities. The US may also grant the MNFC the authority to redistribute logistic resources to meet exigent requirements during an operation. There are strict restrictions, however, on what assets can be redistributed and under what circumstances and nations have the right to withhold specific logistic resources from redistribution.

Control and Coordination Models

The logistic C2 organization of a multinational operation encompasses both the internal logistic staff elements of the MNF headquarters and the overall logistic organization, as integrated into the total MNF C2 structure.

Combined Joint Logistics Officer

If the operation is relatively small or involves only a few multinational partners, the MNFC may rely on the combined-joint logistics officer (CJ-4) and staff, augmented (if necessary) with functional experts, to plan and coordinate MNF logistic activities.

Multinational Joint Logistic Center

In the case of larger, more complex operations requiring more coordination and common support, the MNFC may establish a separate organization to assist the CJ-4 in developing and executing the operation's logistic support plan. NATO designates such an organization for coordinating and managing MNF logistics such as a multinational joint logistic center.

CONCLUSION

This publication expands upon the general logistic guidance contained in JP 3-16, *Multinational Operations,* and provides detailed guidance to US commanders and logisticians involved with providing or receiving logistic support during multinational operations.

CHAPTER I
OVERVIEW

"The man who goes alone can start today; but he who travels with another must wait until that other is ready."

Henry David Thoreau, American writer (1817-1862)

1. Introduction

a. The purpose of this publication is to expand upon the general logistic guidance contained in Joint Publication (JP) 3-16, *Multinational Operations*, and to provide detailed guidance to US commanders and logisticians involved with providing or receiving logistic support during multinational operations. Throughout this publication, the term "multinational" encompasses operations that may also be referred to as "allied," "alliance," "bilateral," "combined," "multilateral," or "coalition." The overall logistics doctrine for supporting US joint operations has been established in JP 4-0, *Joint Logistics.*

b. Logistic support during multinational operations differs from unilateral joint operations in that the participating nations represent different national and military objectives, cultures, and approaches to logistic support. This impacts how the US organizes, prepares, and executes logistic support during multinational operations. A significant challenge in multinational logistics (MNL) involves establishing effective command and control (C2) processes that are acceptable to all troop contributing nations. Logistics is a Service and national responsibility, and under a North Atlantic Treaty Organization (NATO) operation, it is deemed a collective responsibility.

c. The US is a member of various alliances and coalitions. An alliance is the relationship that results from a formal agreement (such as a treaty) between two or more nations for broad, long-term objectives that further the common interests of the members. An example of an alliance is NATO. A coalition is an ad hoc arrangement between two or more nations for common actions. Many coalitions are formed under the guidance of the United Nations (UN). The American, British, Canadian, Australian, and New Zealand (ABCA) Armies Program is a coalition of English speaking nations that have developed logistic doctrine and procedures for supporting multinational operations.

d. When participating in multinational operations, US forces will normally conform to previously approved international agreements. Alliances usually have developed a degree of standardization with regard to administrative, logistic, and operational procedures. The mechanisms for this standardization are international standardization agreements (ISAs). ISAs can be materiel or non-materiel in nature. Materiel ISAs are implemented into the equipment design, development, or adaptation processes to facilitate standardization. Non-materiel related ISAs should already be incorporated into US joint and Service doctrine and tactics, techniques, and procedures. In NATO and allied publications, ISAs are known as standardization agreements (STANAGs) and are instruments used to establish commonality in procedures and equipment. For ABCA these agreements are referred to as quadripartite standing agreements. The existence of these ISAs does not mean that they will be automatically used during a multinational operation. Their use should be clearly specified in the operation plan (OPLAN) or operation order (OPORD). In addition, these ISAs cannot be used as vehicles for obligating financial resources or transferring resources.

2. Multinational Logistics

a. MNL is any coordinated logistic activity involving two or more nations supporting a multinational force (MNF) under the auspices of an alliance or coalition. This includes operations conducted under a UN mandate. MNL includes activities involving both logistic units provided by participating nations designated for use by the multinational force commander (MNFC) as well as a variety of MNL support arrangements that may be developed and used by participating forces.

b. **Requirement for Multinational Logistics.** Throughout its history the US has often acted militarily with multinational partners. Figure I-1 lists selected multinational operations since 2001 in which the US has participated either as the lead nation (LN) or as a significant force contributor. An LN is one nation that assumes the responsibility for procuring and providing a broad spectrum of logistic support for all or a part of the MNF or headquarters (HQ). Compensation or reimbursement will then be subject to agreements between the parties involved. The LN may also assume the responsibility to coordinate logistics of the other nations within its functional and regional responsibility. The requirement for MNL has increased as a result of several factors:

(1) Increasing deployments to distant, logistically austere operational areas to counter a larger array of national security threats;

(2) More diverse composition of MNFs;

(3) High operational tempo and the requirement for multiple simultaneous, overlapping, and/or closely sequential operations that place a heavy burden on logistic force structure; and

(4) Requirements for rapid force deployment with reduced logistic footprints in the operational area.

SELECTED MULTINATIONAL OPERATIONS				
Year	Operation	Location	Type	Command
2001	ENDURING FREEDOM	Afghanistan	Global war on terrorism	US-led coalition
2003	IRAQI FREEDOM / NEW DAWN	Iraq	Regime change, counterinsurgency, stability operations	United Nations (UN)-sanctioned, US-led coalition
2009	OCEAN SHIELD	Indian Ocean	Counterpiracy	North Atlantic Treaty Organization (NATO)-led
2010	UNIFIED RESPONSE	Haiti	Humanitarian relief	US-bilateral
2011	TOMODACHI	Japan	Humanitarian relief	US-bilateral
2011	UNIFIED PROTECTOR	Libya	No-fly zone	UN-sanctioned, NATO-led

Figure I-1. Selected Multinational Operations

c. **Benefits of Multinational Logistics**

(1) JP 3-16, *Multinational Operations,* discusses the importance of international rationalization, standardization, and interoperability for achieving practical cooperation, efficient use of procurement, support, and production resources, and effective multinational operational capability without sacrificing US operational capabilities.

(2) Use of MNL, in the form of centralized coordination, management of common-user logistics (CUL) activities, MNF support arrangements, acquisition and cross-servicing agreement (ACSA), may:

(a) Enhance the ability of the US and its multinational partners to deploy and sustain forces.

(b) Increase operational flexibility and enhance logistic sustainment of the force.

(c) Enable more effective use of intratheater resources through host-nation support (HNS) and theater support contracting. It can especially minimize undesirable competition for contracted support in regions where the local economy and infrastructure have been degraded. Such competition can stress local populations and cause price escalations, reduced availability, quality of local goods, services, and result in the inefficient distribution of resources.

(d) Provide opportunities for nations without sufficient logistic resources to participate in the operation.

(e) Allow nations to provide logistical support instead of forces, when it fits national policies.

(f) Foster bilateral or multilateral support arrangements that lessen demand on the US to provide full support to forces from organic resources. The use of HNS and theater support contracting can lead to significant cost savings and reduced logistic force structure in the operational area.

(3) The extent to which MNL is required and effectively used depends on many factors, to include:

(a) The mission and size of the force,

(b) The extent of multinational diversity and the relative size of national force contributions,

(c) The degree of standardization and interoperability within the force,

(d) The use of a common language and doctrine,

(e) The availability of HNS and theater commercial resources,

(f) The logistic capabilities of participating nations, and

(g) Legal restrictions on exchanging mutual support.

d. A national "go-it-alone" approach to logistics where a participating nation, independent of all other participants, would deploy, arrange support from foreign nations, and compete for theater commercial resources to sustain its national contingents, could lead to logistic chaos and an unbalanced support structure.

e. Multinational operations of even modest complexity require some centralized coordination of logistics and the use of mutual support arrangements to facilitate smooth, timely, responsive, and effective deployment and force sustainment. This may include negotiation of HNS and agreements relating to border crossings, customs and duty fees, medical support, civil engineering, contracting, movement control, and provision of CUL supplies, such as bulk petroleum. See JP 4-0, *Joint Logistics,* for additional information on CUL.

3. The Joint Logistics Environment in Multinational Operations

a. The joint logistics environment, described in JP 4-0, *Joint Logistics*, is also applicable to multinational operations. Operations are distributed and conducted rapidly and simultaneously across multiple operational areas within a single theater or across boundaries of more than one geographic combatant commander (GCC) and can involve a variety of military, interagency, nongovernmental organizations (NGOs), commercial, and multinational partners. The joint logistics environment exists within this operational environment and consists of the conditions, circumstances, and influences that affect the employment of logistic capabilities. It exists at the strategic, operational, and tactical levels of war. Understanding the joint logistics environment and its characteristics is essential to planning, executing, and controlling logistic operations.

(1) **Physical Domains.** MNL takes place within the physical domains of air, land, maritime, and space. Service components provide the expertise within these domains and the MNFC and staff focus on leveraging and integrating those capabilities.

(2) **Information Environment.** The global dispersion of the MNF, the rapidity with which threats arise, and the increased use of capabilities in cyberspace have made real-time or near real-time information critical to support military operations, planning, and MNL execution. Compatibility of networks is essential for providing the MNFC with information to assess MNL and make crucial decisions concerning MNL operations. Additionally, protected access to networks is imperative to sustain MNF readiness and allow rapid and precise response to meet MNFC requirements.

b. **Levels of War.** MNL spans all levels of war. It is, however, at the tactical level where the principal outcome—sustained logistic readiness—of MNL is best measured.

(1) **Strategic.** At the strategic level, MNL is characterized by the vast capacity of the Nation's industrial base, both government and commercial. The Nation's ability to project and sustain military power comes from the strategic level; it enables sustained

military operations over time and represents one of our Nation's greatest strengths. At this level, modern, clearly defined, well-understood and outcome-focused processes should drive effectiveness across the Department of Defense (DOD), multinational, interagency, and commercial organizations. These processes combined with agile force positioning are fundamental to optimizing MNL and are critical to the Nation's ability to maintain flexibility in the face of constantly changing threats.

(2) **Operational.** At the operational level, MNL has its most significant impact. It is at the operational level that strategic and tactical capabilities, processes, and requirements intersect, and it is here where the essence of MNL resides. Multinational logisticians at this level integrate or coordinate national, DOD, combatant command, Service and functional components, multinational partners, interagency, and HNS, with the MNFC's tactical requirements. Logisticians face their greatest challenge at the operational level because of the difficulty of coordinating and integrating capabilities from many providers.

(3) **Tactical.** At the tactical level, logistic support is nation and Service-oriented and executed. Organizations operating at the tactical level are focused on executing assigned tasks to achieve military objectives. Tactical units require sustained logistic readiness to meet assigned objectives. Sustained logistic readiness results from the cumulative efforts of national or Service, agency, and other providers across the entire joint logistics environment.

c. **Global Relationships.** MNL is bound together by a web of relationships among global logistic providers, supporting and supported organizations and units, and other entities. The key global providers for the US are the Services, the Defense Logistics Agency (DLA), and United States Transportation Command (USTRANSCOM). Effective MNL depends on clear roles, responsibilities, and relationships between the global providers. Global providers manage end-to-end processes that provide capabilities to the supported combatant commander (CCDR), and are challenged to link the CCDR requirements to the outcomes of those processes.

4. Logistics Imperatives

a. The value of logistics can be determined by how well the force is deployed and sustained. Three logistic imperatives help determine this: unity of effort, joint logistics enterprise-wide visibility, and rapid and precise response. These imperatives define the desired attributes of a multitiered matrix of key global logistics systems, processes, and organizations that effectively adapt within a complex and fluid environment to meet the emerging needs of the supported CCDR.

(1) **Unity of Effort.** To achieve unity of effort multinational logisticians should develop a clear understanding of how joint and multinational logistic processes work; know the roles and responsibilities of the providers executing tasks in those processes; build agreement around common measures of performance (process outcomes); and provide appropriate members of the joint force visibility into the processes.

(2) **Joint Logistics Environment—Multinational-Wide Visibility.** Multinational-wide visibility requires timely and accurate information regarding the logistic

processes, resources, and requirements of member nations. This allows commanders and their staffs to gain the knowledge necessary to make effective recommendations and decisions. Visibility fundamentally answers the CCDR's questions: Where is it? How will it get there? When will it get there?

(3) **Rapid and Precise Response.** Rapid and precise response is the ability of core logistic capabilities, military and commercial, to meet the constantly changing needs of the MNF. The effectiveness of MNL can be measured by assessing the following attributes, or key performance indicators:

(a) Speed is at the core of responsiveness. Speed does not mean everything moves at the same rate or fastest rate, but everything moves according to priority at the rate that produces the most effective support to the MNF.

(b) Reliability is characterized by a high degree of predictability of the global providers to deliver required support to the supported commander.

(c) Efficiency is directly related to the amount of resources required to deliver a specific outcome. In the tactical and operational environments, inefficiency increases the logistic footprint and increases force protection (FP) requirements and risk. At the strategic level, inefficiency increases the cost for a unit of process outcome.

b. These logistics imperatives enable the measurement of our ability to provide sustained logistic readiness.

5. Multinational Logistics Principles

a. The principles of logistics for US joint operations, described in JP 4-0, *Joint Logistics*, also apply to the logistics of multinational operations. However, because participating forces represent sovereign nations, there are several unique principles for MNL operations. Figure I-2 lists the principles of MNL as contained in NATO's logistic publication Military Committee (MC) 319/2, *NATO Principles and Policies for Logistics*, and expanded upon in Allied Joint Publication (AJP)-4, *Allied Joint Logistic Doctrine*. Although first formulated in NATO documents, these principles are adaptable to all multinational operations.

(1) **Collective Responsibility.** Participating nations and the MNFC have a collective responsibility for the logistics in support of multinational operations. Although nations are ultimately responsible for the support of their forces, logistic support in multinational military operations is not solely a national responsibility. This collective responsibility encourages partner nations (PNs) to cooperatively share the provision and use of logistic capabilities and resources to support the force effectively and efficiently. Standardization, cooperation, and multinationality in logistics build together the basis for flexible and efficient use of logistic support, thereby contributing to the operational success.

(2) **Authority.** Sovereign nations are reluctant to give MNFCs directive authority for logistics. There is an essential interdependence between responsibility and authority. The responsibility assigned to any MNFC should be matched with the delegation of authority

```
┌─────────────────────────────────────────────────────────────────────┐
│ Logistics Principles of Multinational Operations                      │
│                                                                       │
│ Per MC 319/2 the NATO principles and      Per Joint Publication 4-0 principles and │
│ policies for logistics are*:              policies for logistics include**: │
│   • Collective responsibility               • Economy                 │
│   • Authority                               • Simplicity              │
│   • Primacy of operational requirements     • Flexibility             │
│   • Cooperation                             • Responsiveness          │
│   • Coordination                            • Survivability           │
│   • Assured provision                       • Sustainability          │
│   • Sufficiency                             • Attainability           │
│   • Efficiency                                                        │
│   • Flexibility                                                       │
│   • Visibility and transparency                                       │
│   • Synergy                                                           │
│   • Simplicity                                                        │
│   • Timeliness                                                        │
│   *Principles listed in NATO Publication MC 319/2, NATO Principles and Policies for │
│    Logistics, and in Allied Joint Publication (AJP)-4, Allied Joint Logistic Doctrine. │
│   **Principles listed in Joint Publication 4-0, Joint Logistics, as well as MC 319/2 and AJP-4. │
│ Legend                                                                │
│ MC  Military Committee         NATO  North Atlantic Treaty Organization │
└─────────────────────────────────────────────────────────────────────┘
```

Figure I-2. Logistics Principles of Multinational Operations

by PNs to allow the adequate discharge of responsibilities. The MNFC, at the appropriate level, must be given sufficient authority over the logistic resources necessary to receive, employ, sustain, and re-deploy assigned forces in the most effective manner. (See Chapter III, "Multinational Logistic Planning," for more details regarding MNFC authorities.)

(3) **Primacy of Operational Requirements.** Logistic support is focused on accomplishing the mission, as defined by the MNFC and participating nations. Nations should provide sufficient logistic assets to support the MNFC's operational objectives.

(4) **Cooperation.** Nations should cooperate with each other and with the MNFC to achieve unity of effort so that their forces and the overall operation are adequately supported. The basis for this begins in peacetime with the establishment of bilateral/multilateral contacts and agreements. Applied across the full spectrum of logistics, including between the civilian and military sector within and between nations, it contributes to the best use of limited resources.

(5) **Coordination.** Nations should closely coordinate their logistic actions with the MNFC throughout both the planning and execution phases of the operation. This coordination should exist between all levels of the operational and logistical command structure. Generic and standing pre-arranged agreements help facilitate logistic coordination and cooperation. Coordination is especially important in the areas of movement control, contracting, medical support, customs and border clearance, negotiation and allocation of HNS, provision of fuel supply, and negotiation of bilateral and multilateral agreements.

(6) **Assured Provision.** Nations should ensure, individually or collectively, the provision of logistic resources to support forces allocated to the MNF during peace, crisis, and conflict.

(7) **Sufficiency.** Logistic support of an MNF should be sufficient to achieve designated levels of readiness, sustainability, and mobility to meet operational requirements. The provisioning of support to participating forces and the overall operation may be accomplished individually or by cooperative arrangements among the participants.

(8) **Efficiency.** See subparagraph 4a(3)(c).

(9) **Flexibility.** Logistics should be proactive, adaptable, and responsive to achieve the mission. Adequate and timely logistic planning, which considers potentially changing circumstances, enhances flexibility. Since the scope, mission, and composition of multinational operations differ, logistic support should be tailored to meet operational requirements unique to each operation.

(10) **Visibility and Transparency.** Visibility and transparency of logistic resources is essential for planning effective logistic support and managing it accordingly. Common reporting formats should be provided to participants and interoperable information technologies employed for rapidly passing and processing logistic information.

(11) **Synergy.** The coordination of logistics capabilities enables the US and other participating nations to build logistics capacity to support operations more effectively with fewer overall resources.

(12) **Simplicity.** To be effective, the logistic support concept and its implementation should be easily understood. Simplified reporting requirements and formats should be employed. GCCs should pursue efforts to achieve interoperability with likely multinational partners during peacetime as part of their theater campaign plan.

(13) **Timeliness.** Developing and establishing an effective logistic framework requires more time in multinational operations than for unilateral operations because of the involvement of multiple nations in the planning process.

b. In addition to the MNL principles listed above, several other "principles of logistics," identified in JP 4-0, *Joint Logistics,* and not unique to multinational operations, are also applicable.

(1) **Responsiveness.** The logistic support of an MNF must be responsive to rapidly changing operational circumstances. This requires planning and standardization far in advance of the operation and facilitates the exchange of common support items among the forces.

(2) **Survivability.** In today's world of diverse threats FP measures should be considered when establishing MNL arrangements.

(3) **Sustainability.** Long-term support can be enhanced through use of MNL, either individually or by the kinds of cooperative arrangements discussed in Chapter III, "Multinational Logistic Planning."

(4) **Attainability.** MNL can be used to achieve minimum essential levels of support quickly since it relies on more sources of support than just national resources.

(5) **Economy.** Given the limits on logistic resources and the benefits of reducing logistic footprints in the operational area, nations should work together to achieve the most economic use of logistic resources through multinational coordination and mutual support arrangements.

6. Special Considerations in Organizing and Conducting Multinational Logistic Operations

a. **The Impact of National Sovereignty.** The planning and conduct of logistics in operations involving multiple sovereign nations characteristically differs from that in unilateral operations.

(1) MNFCs typically do not have the same degree of directive authority over MNF logistics as commanders of national operations. Nations give MNFCs only as much authority over their national logistic resources as they are willing to concede to achieve national objectives in the operation. As described in Chapter III, "Multinational Logistic Planning," these authorities are generally quite limited, and often involve only coordinating authority. As a result, effective logistic operations in a multinational operation depend on personal relationships between multinational and national force commanders. MNFCs and the logistic staff use persuasion and diplomacy to encourage national contingents to support MNF operational priorities. In order to ensure better understanding between commanders, liaison officers should be dispatched to all relevant organizations throughout the multinational C2 structure.

(2) US and other forces participating in multinational operations operate under limitations imposed by applicable international agreements, including status-of-forces agreements (SOFAs), national laws, and regulations. The US has negotiated a number of bilateral SOFAs that govern US forces operating within another nation's territory. SOFAs may also be multilateral and should be negotiated to apply to all participants in the MNF. Detailed SOFA provisions are usually contained in supporting technical arrangements (TAs). Many of the areas addressed in the TAs relate directly to logistic issues: medical support, environmental obligations, customs and duties, movement control, landing rights and/or port utilization fees, and rights and protection of MNF contractors. Accordingly, the MNFC's logistic and legal staffs may become closely involved with negotiation, implementation, and application of the SOFA and TAs to ensure that such documents facilitate rather than hinder logistic support of the operation.

(3) Differences in national rules of engagement and FP requirements constitute potential areas of friction in a multinational operation and could affect the security of operating bases and logistic assets that US forces and MNFs rely on.

(4) National laws guide the exchange of logistic support among nations. There are a number of legal provisions that stipulate the manner in which US forces can exchange logistic support with other force contingents and/or participate in MNL arrangements. (See Appendix C, "Relevant Legal Authorities for United States Logistics in Support of Multinational Operations," for a more complete discussion of this subject.)

b. **The US as Provider and Recipient of Logistic Support.** US national security strategy envisions that the US may provide logistic support as part of its national contribution to a multinational operation, as it did in Operations RESTORE HOPE (Somalia), UPHOLD DEMOCRACY (Haiti), and STABILIZE (East Timor). The US in turn could require extensive foreign logistic assistance (as in Operations DESERT SHIELD/STORM, ongoing Balkan peacekeeping operations, and ENDURING FREEDOM/IRAQI FREEDOM). The US, therefore, is likely to be both a consumer and provider of CUL in multinational operations. US commanders and logistic planners should view MNL as a means to effectively and efficiently support US forces.

c. **Differences in Multinational Logistics Based on Organizational Structure.** JP 3-16, *Multinational Operations*, lists two basic types of multinational operations—alliance and coalition—and describes the general command structures associated with each. Each type of operation has distinctive characteristics that affect the logistics C2 relationships, funding and reimbursement mechanisms for MNL support, and the scope of MNL arrangements.

(1) **Alliance Operations.** Alliance operations are conducted within the political context of a formal agreement between two or more nations that are united by treaty in the promotion and defense of common security interests.

(a) Figure I-3 summarizes logistics-related characteristics of types of multinational operations. Although these characteristics may apply generally to regional alliances and may serve to facilitate logistic support planning and execution, their specific application in actual operations may not be clearly established, as was discovered during the early stages of Operation JOINT ENDEAVOR in Bosnia-Herzegovina in 1996. (At the beginning of this operation some participating nations maintained that NATO's collective logistic doctrine did not apply to non-Article 5 operations—that is, those operations not involving the defense of NATO territory. This issue was resolved in an update of MC 319/2, *NATO Principles and Policies for Logistics*, which specifically now applies to all NATO operations.)

(b) In addition, in today's strategic environment—which encourages broad multilateral participation—alliance operations often include non-alliance members, as is the case in NATO peacekeeping operations in the Balkans. Within NATO operations, forces of non-alliance nations must be certified as logistically supportable in order to ensure that such contingents possess adequate logistics capabilities prior to being incorporated into the operation. Support arrangements need not be strictly national. Non-NATO nations can make arrangements with NATO and other nations for the provision of selected CUL support, as Russia has done with the US in Kosovo. However, whatever the source, the logistic support of non-alliance members needs to be integrated into the alliance's overall concept of support.

LOGISTICS-RELATED CHARACTERISTICS OF TYPES OF MULTINATIONAL OPERATIONS				
	Alliance Operations	United Nations (UN) Operations	US-Led Coalition	Non-US-Led Coalition
Logistic command and control structure/ organization	Established organization and relationships. Tailored for specific operations. Frequently exercised.	UN force commander has no logistic authority over troop contributions and logistic resources.	As arranged among participating nations.	As arranged among participating nations.
Logistic doctrine and procedures	North Atlantic Treaty Organization (NATO): Well developed. Highly detailed. Commonly agreed.	Developed but unfamiliar to many participating countries.	US uses national doctrine. Familiar to some participants and shares many features with established alliance doctrine.	Varies, depending on lead nation and participating nations. (American, British, Canadian, Australian Armies' Program nations have agreed logistics guidelines).
Division of logistic responsibility	Nations and NATO have collective responsibility for logistic support. Member nations are ultimately responsible for deploying and supporting their own forces, but encouraged to use multinational logistics arrangements.	UN is responsible for planning and coordinating logistic support of UN-commanded operations. Troop contributing nations are encouraged to provide units with organic unit level logistics capability. Nations must confirm authorized contingent structure and logistic support in a contingent-owned equipment memorandum of understanding. UN sometimes requests US and other nations to provide logistic support for UN contingents. UN responsible for base camp infrastructure and mission support.	US coordinates logistic support. Participating nations are responsible for own logistic support unless otherwise negotiated. Level of logistic integration is operation-specific.	Lead nation coordinates logistic support. Participating nations are responsible for own logistic support unless otherwise negotiated. Level of logistic integration is operation-specific.
Commander's logistic authorities	NATO: Generally agreed-upon authorities and responsibilities for managing and coordinating deployment and sustainment functions.	UN force commander has no logistic authority over troop contributions and logistic resources.	As arranged among participating nations.	As arranged among participating nations.
Operational logistic planning	Structured planning process. Established multinational planning staffs. Highly integrated.	Structured planning process with some pre-planning. However, limited UN headquarters planning capability. Small permanent staff. Relies on augmented military staff provided by member states.	US planning process and staff with augmentation and input from selected participants.	Lead nation planning process and staff. Major US contribution.

Figure I-3. Logistics-Related Characteristics of Types of Multinational Operations

LOGISTICS-RELATED CHARACTERISTICS OF TYPES OF MULTINATIONAL OPERATIONS (cont'd)				
Logistic requirements determination	Detailed requirements determination process in support of force structure and operational planning.	Some operation-specific requirements planning. No peacetime force structure planning.	Detailed operational requirements planning for national forces. Ad hoc integration for coalition requirements. Some coordinated force planning with selected nations.	Depends on lead nation. US typically coordinates closely with lead nation and selected participants.
Standardization interoperability	High level for logistic doctrine and procedures. Low-medium level for logistics supplies and equipment. Formal developed standardization agreements in a broad range of logistic functions.	Low level for logistic doctrine and procedures, logistic supplies and equipment. No formal standardization agreements.	Varies depending on participants. Medium-high level in some areas with close allies.	Varies depending on participants.
Knowledge of participant logistic capability/ experience in operating with participants	High. Lesser experience with non-alliance countries participating in alliance operations.	Low-medium depending on participants.	Low-high depending on participants. Usually some close allies involved.	Low-high depending on participants.
Logistic infrastructure to support operations	Extensive Alliance-funded structure.	UN-owned logistic base and some major equipment items.	Nationally owned.	Nationally owned.
Host-nation support	NATO: Established agreements with alliance members. NATO commanders coordinate and negotiate on behalf of nations.	UN force commander negotiates with host nation.	Varies depending on operation's bilateral process or nations may give multinational force commander (MNFC) authority to negotiate.	Varies depending on operation's bilateral process or nations may give MNFC authority to negotiate.
Funding	NATO: Common funding for headquarters and approved projects that benefit the alliance or the operation as a whole. Otherwise, nations responsible for all operational costs.	Troop contributing nations partially reimbursed for national troops, equipment, and logistic sustainment. Nations providing logistic support to other participants through letters of assistance may be reimbursed for expenses.	Participating nations normally pay own costs. Terms of multinational support determined by nations. Nations may financially assist less-capable participants.	Participating nations normally pay own costs. Terms of multinational support determined by nations. Nations may financially assist less-capable participants.

Figure I-3. Logistics-Related Characteristics of Types of Multinational Operations (cont'd)

(2) **Coalition.** A coalition is an arrangement between two or more nations for common action. Coalitions can form within the framework of a formal international organization (such as the UN) or through one of the nations in the coalition (possibly building off peacetime coalition structures, such as the ABCA forum).

(a) **UN Operations.** These operations are conducted under the authority of a UN Security Council resolution and under the leadership of a UN military force commander who may report to a Special Representative of the Secretary-General. The UN has no standing army or police force of its own, and member states are asked to contribute military and police personnel required for each operation. Every member state is legally obligated to pay their respective share toward peacekeeping in accordance with the provisions of Article 17 of the Charter of the UN. Peacekeeping soldiers are paid by their own governments according to their own national rank and salary scale. Countries volunteering uniformed personnel to peacekeeping operations are reimbursed by the UN at a flat rate as approved by the General Assembly. US participation in UN operations in Somalia, Haiti, and East Timor are examples of this model. UN operations are characterized by the following:

1. They are conducted in accordance with UN policies, regulations, and procedures, which may not be familiar to CCDRs.

2. Standardization or interoperability among troop contingents may be low due to the diverse mix of participating nations and lack of pre-operational multinational training.

3. UN operations are more likely to be ad hoc than operations conducted by regional alliances.

4. Participants and their logistic capabilities can vary widely, although some nations specialize in UN operations and have substantial experience operating with other participating nations.

5. UN HQ is responsible for establishing a UN field logistic system to support the UN force during all phases of the operation. Nations are encouraged, however, to provide forces that are logistically self-sufficient, and that confirm logistic arrangements with the UN.

(b) **US-Led Coalition Operations.** US-led coalition operations may be authorized by the UN, but the logistic organizational relationships, doctrine, and procedures are generally based upon US doctrine. The overall C2 structure may be one of the types discussed in JP 3-16, *Multinational Operations*. US-led coalition operations are characterized by the following:

1. The organizational structure for coordinating and managing MNL activities is an extension of the US logistic organization. Consequently, the core MNF HQ logistic staff consists primarily of US Service members, although it is augmented by coalition members.

2. The degree of standardization or interoperability among coalition members depends upon the coalition partners involved in the specific operation. US-led coalitions, however, will typically include a few close allies that frequently operate with US forces and thus are familiar with US logistic doctrine and procedures. Other coalition partners may have little or no experience operating with US forces.

3. Because of its logistic strengths, the US may be requested to provide a range of common logistic support to some or all participating nations.

4. Depending on the kind of operation, operational planning will be shaped primarily by US objectives and approaches. However, to allow for effective support

of the operation, the US MNFC should work with participating nations to identify logistic support requirements and include them in appropriate logistic plans.

(c) **Non-US-Led Coalition Operations.** The US may participate in coalition operations led by another nation. Such operations have many of the same general characteristics as US-led operations, except US forces are in a subordinate role. In such operations, the LN establishes the parameters for logistic participation. The US joint force commander (JFC) (or separate Service component commanders if there is no joint force command) is guided by applicable US laws, regulations, and established agreements concerning the provision or exchange of logistic support among participants. The US JFC must clearly understand the expectations of the MNFC regarding US contributions to the overall concept of support.

(d) Whatever the structure of the coalition, the nation or international organization that has the lead in organizing the coalition is challenged to rationalize and harmonize the logistic support of the disparate participating countries. The MNFC may direct the use and application of logistic policies and procedures of the sponsoring nation or agency. Considerable ingenuity may be required to articulate policies and procedures throughout the MNF to provide understanding, a common view, and integration of forces and resources.

(3) The variable conditions under which US forces may operate in either an alliance or coalition structure place a premium on developing flexible logistic support concepts that can be tailored to effectively respond to a broad range of contingencies. Regardless of the method of employment, US forces participating in multinational operations must adhere to US laws as well as to appropriate international agreements.

d. **Impact on Multinational Logistics by Type of Operation.** JP 3-16, *Multinational Operations*, lists the variety of multinational operations in which Armed Forces of the United States may be involved, ranging from the extremes of major operations and campaigns to the vast variety of crisis response and limited contingency operations; military engagement, security cooperation, and deterrence activities often helps keep the day-to-day tensions between nations or groups below the threshold of armed conflict. The nature of the military mission dictates both the extent and type of MNL support required.

(1) **Logistic Support in Major Operations and Campaigns.** Intensive combat operations result in increased demands upon medical capabilities and medical evacuations; all classes of supply, especially fuel and ammunition; battle damage repair capabilities; replacement of major end items/principal items of equipment; spare parts; and transportation. Intense combat operations involving an MNF reinforce the requirement for centralized coordination and mutual support arrangements to achieve operationally efficient support. Reimbursement is less of an issue; redistribution and reallocation may be more easily authorized.

(2) **Logistic Support in Crisis Response and Limited Contingency Operations.** Many of the missions associated with **crisis response and limited contingency operations,** such as disaster relief and foreign humanitarian assistance operations, will not involve

combat operations or require combat forces. Others, such as Operation RESTORE HOPE in Somalia, can be extremely dangerous and require a significant effort to protect friendly forces while accomplishing the mission; therefore, US forces must be prepared to conduct the full range of military operations in support of multinational military operations. Often, broad multilateral participation is solicited. There is a need for close coordination with intergovernmental organizations (IGOs), NGOs, and local civilian agencies operating within the same areas. The MNFC is likely to be responsible for coordinating operations of the MNF with these organizations and for coordinating selected logistic activities of the force, e.g., contracting, movement control, and engineering.

e. **Multinational Operations.** Multinational operations may sometimes have a nonmilitary dimension (e.g., humanitarian assistance or stability operations). Even when the MNF itself does not have such missions, there may be humanitarian relief or various nation building activities occurring simultaneously in the operational area.

(1) Humanitarian relief operations will typically be conducted by NGOs but may be augmented by government agencies and organizations to include military forces, as was seen with US and Pakistani forces assisting with earthquake relief efforts in Pakistan. IGOs, such as the UN and the Organization for Security and Cooperation in Europe, may be involved in coordinating these and other nonmilitary activities. It is also possible that antiterrorism and other combat operations could occur simultaneously with peacekeeping and humanitarian support operations, with distinct MNFs operating within separate command chains, as in Operation ENDURING FREEDOM in Afghanistan.

(2) **The activities of NGOs and IGOs in the operational area can both complicate and assist logistic support of an MNF.** NGOs are often very familiar with the logistics-related conditions in the operational area—including local sources of supply—and have established contacts with host nations (HNs) and regional contractors. MNF logisticians can take advantage of NGO information and relationships to arrange HNS and theater support contracting and plan logistic operations. On the other hand, NGO activities create additional competing demands for local infrastructure and support resources. Although NGOs can reduce the need for military logistic capabilities (for humanitarian operations) they also could require military logistic support in an emergency. Many NGOs will want to distance themselves from military organizations for fear that it may seem as they are taking sides in a conflict or that being associated with the military will keep people from seeking their help.

(3) It is essential that the activities and capabilities of NGOs and IGOs be factored into planning during MNL efforts and that MNF logisticians maintain close coordination with all such groups throughout all phases of a multinational operation, beginning with early planning. MNFCs will need to establish appropriate organizations for coordination with such groups, and liaison contacts with nations conducting their own civil-military activities independently of the MNF.

(4) **The use of DOD resources in a manner that may directly or indirectly assist or otherwise benefit NGOs and IGOs may result in an Anti-Deficiency Act Violation.** Consultation with the legal advisor throughout the planning process is

recommended to avoid such pitfalls. DOD has limited authority and funding to provide for the transportation of humanitarian relief. Certain authorities, however, such as the Humanitarian and Civic Assistance Act, Title 10, United States Code (USC), Section 401, require the promotion of operational readiness skills of the US military participants and high-level approval. Other authorities, such as Overseas, Humanitarian, Disaster and Civic Assistance, Title 10, USC, Section 2557, do not contain such requirements, but could raise other legal issues depending upon the facts of the individual case. In order to ensure the specific use of DOD resources is authorized and intended to be properly implemented under the correct legal authority, the MNFC should consult with his or her legal staff officer on legal authorities relating to the specific use of DOD resources.

See JP 3-08, Interorganizational Coordination During Joint Operations, *for further details.*

    f. **Force Protection.** FP is as important in multinational operations as in US-only operations but presents special challenges.

        (1) Multinational partners do not necessarily share US views on standards of FP, however, NATO has promulgated AJP-3.14, *Allied Joint Doctrine for Force Protection*, which should be reviewed and used when US joint forces are participating in a NATO operation.

        (2) The risk of fratricide is greater in multinational operations.

        (3) Because of the salient operational and political role of the US in a coalition, US forces may be singled out as targets in a multinational operation.

See JP 3-16, Multinational Operations, *JP 3-07.2,* Antiterrorism, *and JP 3-35,* Deployment and Redeployment Operations, *for further details.*

        (4) Logistic operations are especially vulnerable to terrorist and adversary attack. The self-defense capabilities of logistic units are typically limited. During deployment and redeployment operations, forces are often dispersed and not resourced to provide adequate FP. Requirements also may exist to provide FP for nonmilitary agencies and contractors. Due to these constraints, close liaison and coordination with the MNFC and other coalition participants, including the HN is required.

        (5) Within US-led coalitions, the US MNFC should develop and coordinate FP guidelines and a security plan for the MNF as a whole. FP, however, is ultimately a national responsibility and within national units, national commanders will conduct FP in accordance with both their own national policy and coalition guidelines.

        (6) The FP security plan should include assignment of sufficient FP resources to permit continued logistic operations in support of combat and other mission forces.

        (7) Depending on the complexity of the operation, there may be special requirements for commanders of national support elements (NSEs) to coordinate FP with other partner NSEs and with the MNFC.

(8) Depending on the threat, the US may decide to rely on HN or MNFs for some FP of rear logistic units. Conversely, the US may be requested to provide FP to MNFs transiting or located in the US operational area.

(9) The ability of available medical treatment capabilities to handle mass casualties from chemical, biological, radiological, and nuclear (CBRN) hazards should be assessed and considered during planning. A multinational unit such as a NATO CBRN defense battalion could provide CBRN reconnaissance (including detection and identification) as well as contamination mitigation.

(10) Several DOD organizations perform transportation security infrastructure vulnerability and physical security assessments. For example, the US Navy conducts port integrated vulnerability assessments and the Defense Threat Reduction Agency conducts balanced survivability assessments in accordance with Department of Defense Instruction (DODI) 3000.08, *Balanced Survivability Assessments (BSAs),* and joint staff integrated vulnerability assessments in accordance with DODI 2000.16, *DOD Antiterrorism (AT) Standards.*

g. **Multinational Logistic Operations in a CBRN Environment.** In a CBRN environment, MNL operations can be impacted by hazards produced by enemy, friendly, or neutral actions. Multinational operations increase the incentives for an adversary to, at a minimum, threaten the use of CBRN, as such threats may discourage members of the international community from contributing forces to a multinational operation. Threats or actual CBRN attacks could test multinational FP at all key logistics nodes.

For more detailed information on CBRN impacts and considerations see JP 3-11, Operations in Chemical, Biological, Radiological, and Nuclear (CBRN) Environments.

h. **Limits to Using Multinational Logistics.** Although the use of MNL has substantial benefits, there are limits as to how extensively it can be used.

(1) Most nations lack the deployable logistic assets to support both their own forces and to provide additional logistic units for general support of the MNF.

(2) **Nations may be reluctant to commit logistic forces to support the overall operation early in the force generation process.** This reluctance can complicate timely establishment of MNL arrangements that are crucial for streamlining support and leveraging logistic assets of multinational partners.

(3) **Lack of established MNL planning organizations, especially in coalitions, leads to ad hoc logistic organization development,** which in turn adversely impacts the effectiveness and efficiency of logistic support, especially during initial stages of operations.

(4) Some functional areas (e.g., blood supply and some equipment maintenance) are not conducive to multinational arrangements because of national sensitivities or material incompatibilities.

(5) It is **difficult to achieve multinational consensus** during the planning phase regarding common funding for financing/reimbursement arrangements, yet up-front common funding can significantly reduce critical support costs.

(6) There are many gaps in standardization of procedures, supplies, and equipment, especially among US and non-NATO military forces that impede MNL. Alternative procedures implemented by participating nations are often required to lessen the adverse impact of this lack of standardization. However, understanding where logistics processes can be leveraged collectively will enable complementing actions for unified effort.

(7) In order to minimize differences between US and allied logistics doctrine, joint doctrine provides the US position for developing multinational doctrine with NATO allies and selected multinational partners. This publication, where appropriate, incorporates key MNL doctrine concepts and terminology that is already agreed by the US and multinational partners and that provide a model for emergent situations where no agreed multinational doctrine exists. Differences will remain, however, that could cause confusion and impede MNL operations. Some of the US definitions for the terms differ from the corresponding NATO definitions. For non-US-led multinational operations, US commanders and staff need to review key coalition/alliance terminology before operational planning to ensure common understanding with multinational partners.

(8) MNL C2 structures and mutual support arrangements and executing MNL operations require substantial staff time and effort. However, familiarity with MNL concepts and procedures gained through training and operational experience can substantially reduce the administrative burden of MNL and maximize its benefits.

CHAPTER II
LOGISTIC CAPABILITIES

"There is nothing more common than to find considerations of supply affecting the strategic lines of a campaign and a war."

Carl von Clausewitz, Prussian general and military strategist (1780–1831)

1. Introduction

a. In this chapter, MNL is further described in terms of the capabilities it delivers. The core MNL capabilities are supply, maintenance operations, deployment and distribution, health service support (HSS), engineering, logistic services, and operational contract support. The core MNL capabilities, when combined with multinational personnel service support, provide the ability to globally project and sustain the MNF. Understanding these capabilities will enable MNFCs and their subordinate commanders to obtain effective logistic support. The multinational logistician should work to integrate and make effective use of Service, agency, commercial, interagency, and MNL assets.

b. Because of the diversity among national forces, the opportunities to integrate supply, maintenance, and repair activities on a multinational level are limited. There may be occasions, however, when nations participating in an operation are using equipment procured from another participating nation. Even if integration is limited, developing complementing logistics actions will assist with unity of effort. Logistic planners should identify equipment similarities among participating nations during the planning or force generation process. In these situations, operation planners should be apprised of such considerations in assigning forces to specific commands or areas, for example, basing all allied F-16 aircraft at the same operational area in close proximity. Logistic planners should also identify areas where international agreements would facilitate supply and maintenance support of multinational operations. Upon identifying a need, the MNFC should seek a determination of the feasibility of such agreements and, where applicable, pursue their development in coordination with the appropriate higher command level. It is possible that the logistic footprint of participating nations may be reduced by such initiatives.

See AJP-4, Allied Joint Logistic Doctrine, *for more details.*

2. Supply Operations

a. Logisticians integrate the three functional capabilities of managing supplies and equipment, managing inventory, and managing supplier networks within the supply core logistic capability. Visibility of requirements and demands is critical for supplies and it requires communication and integration with other areas affecting the supply chain, maintenance, and distribution. Specifically, supply demand planning involves the MNF operation planners, maintenance operations, and the distribution system to fully consider major components of the logistics pipeline beyond commodity stockpiles. Demand planning is accomplished in a collaborative environment to provide responsive supply operations.

Another focus area critical to effective supply operations is the return and retrograde of equipment and supplies. Both demand planning and return and retrograde functions involve collaboration and execution by all three areas of the supply chain.

b. **Manage Supplies and Equipment.** Nations have the ultimate responsibility for ensuring the provision of sufficient supplies and services to adequately sustain their forces in multinational operations. However, under the premise that nations and MNFCs share a collective responsibility for the logistics in support of multinational operations, the MNFC will have the control of the use of commonly funded supplies and services. Integrated supply operations capitalize on supplier network performance capabilities and the integrated links with the supporting distribution and maintenance systems.

(1) Multinational support agreements and arrangements can usually be considered for the provision of food, water (bulk and bottled), bulk fuel, some ammunition types and medical supplies. The supplies and services to be provided by MNL will be determined in concert with nations prior to commencement of the operation and will depend on the degree of standardization and interoperability within the force. This should be determined during the logistic and HNS planning conferences. Possible methods of multinational provision are given in NATO publication AJP-4.9, *Modes of Multinational Support*.

(2) The stock criteria in terms of days of supply will be determined based on the sustainability statement, agreed by participating nations for the particular operation, and published in the logistic annex to the OPORD. Stocks for sustained operations will include organic stocks of units plus additional stocks, maintained at support levels, necessary to cover the order and shipping time for supplies. The actual positioning of supplies will be dependent on the operational situation and the ability of the strategic and tactical transport to move supplies forward into the operational area. There are two basic methods of operating the supply system:

(a) **"Push"-System.** The logistic organization operates a "push"-system when the replenishment is based on anticipated requirements or standard consumption rates. Generally, in such a system, the supplies are shipped (pushed) as far as possible to the customer. To avoid the creation of large stockpiles seamless coordination between operational and logistic planners is required as well as effective use of technology such as command, control, and information systems and asset tracking systems.

(b) **"Pull"-System.** The logistic organization operates a "pull"-system when the resupply is based on requisitions from the supported unit. Under specific conditions this system may offer economic advantages, but when contact with the enemy is imminent, a lower risk approach may be needed, due especially to the time constraints.

(c) Under both of these methods, supplies may be distributed by supply point, unit distribution, or a combination of both. Supply point distribution moves supplies to a central distribution point where receiving units arrange their own delivery. Unit distribution describes a delivery system, which moves supplies forward to the user unit, eliminating the individual unit delivery arrangement requirement.

(d) In practice, an amalgamation of all existing methods will be used to support a combined/multinational operation and will vary for each campaign and phase of operation. Nations and commanders will have to adapt and compromise, creating an efficient supply chain and an effective regeneration loop. Other factors that will influence stock levels and locations include the diplomatic and political situations, the risk to which the stocks will be exposed, and the cost effectiveness of holding stocks forward versus resupplying stocks from home bases.

(3) Supply transactions between nations or national forces may take the form of pre-planned logistic assistance, emergency logistic assistance in crisis and conflict, multinational support, or redistribution. The compensation for delivered or redistributed supplies should be executed in accordance with procedures agreed upon by the PNs. Nations should implement the provisions of these agreements in their national doctrine and procedures to enhance the efficient execution of mutual support.

See Chapter III, "Multinational Logistic Planning," for more information.

3. Maintenance Operations

a. Maintenance operations deliver systems readiness for the MNFC. Each member nation executes maintenance as a core logistic capability to maintain the fleet readiness of units and capabilities.

b. In crisis or conflict, an efficient maintenance organization, composed of MNF and national repair facilities, is an essential component of MNF's capability. Therefore, nations should be encouraged to make bilateral and multilateral agreements in peace to cover use of national repair facilities in both peacetime and wartime. This facilitates the transfer of repair loads from one nation's facilities to another and will exercise cross-servicing facilities and procedures. Whenever weapon systems are used by more than one nation, a coordinated approach to logistics is recommended. Not only can logistic resources be shared, but also by consolidating supply and maintenance requirements, unique opportunities are created to reduce investment and operating costs.

4. Deployment and Distribution

a. The global dispersion of the threats, combined with the necessity to rapidly deploy, execute, and sustain operations worldwide makes the deployment and distribution capability the cornerstone of MNL. This global distribution-based system requires the end-to-end synchronization of all elements of distribution. The deployment and distribution capability supports the movement of forces and unit equipment during the deployment and redeployment processes, and supports materiel movement during the sustainment of operations. Asset and in-transit visibility provides the CCDR the capability to see and redirect strategic and operational commodity and force flow in support of current and projected priorities.

See JP 3-35, Deployment and Redeployment Operations, and JP 4-09, Distribution Operations, for additional information.

b. **Move the Force.** The Joint Staff Operations Directorate, as the joint deployment process owner, serves as the DOD focal point to improve the deployment process supporting multinational operations, and interagency coordination. Force providers are supported by USTRANSCOM during the planning and execution of the deployment and redeployment process. USTRANSCOM, as the distribution process owner, supports the deployment process by providing the strategic distribution capability to move forces and materiel in support of MNFC operational requirements and to return personnel, equipment, and materiel to home and/or demobilization stations.

c. **Movement Control.** A variety of organizations may be established to manage, control, and coordinate strategic and operational movement for multinational operations.

(1) In US-led multinational operations, the movement control concept is usually an extension of US joint doctrine, as discussed in JP 3-35, *Deployment and Redeployment Operations,* and JP 4-09, *Distribution Operations.*

(2) The organization and planning tools for synchronizing and coordinating movement control during multinational operations and in other kinds of multinational operations are similar, and will usually include:

(a) A planning center (at the strategic or geographic command level) to construct a detailed multinational deployment plan.

(b) A joint movement coordination center at the MNF HQ level.

(c) An air component center for controlling air movements.

(d) Organizational elements for managing/coordinating reception, staging, onward movement, and integration (RSOI) activities to coordinate MNF movements with the HN's national movement coordination center, if established and allocating any common-user transportation resources.

(3) In a NATO operation, for example, strategic movement is managed by the allied movement coordination center (AMCC), which combines and deconflicts separate national detailed deployment plans (DDPs) into a single multinational deployment plan to ensure smooth flow of forces in accordance with the MNFC's deployment priorities. The AMCC, in cooperation with NATO's civil transportation planning boards and committees, also assist nations in resolving strategic lift shortfalls through arrangements with other allied nations and/or commercial transportation firms. See AJP-3.13, *Allied Joint Doctrine for the Deployment of Forces.*

(4) At the operational level, a joint theater movement staff (JTMS) develops movement and transportation directives and plans, and recommends priorities for theater movement requirements. A joint transportation coordination center (JTCC) may also be established. The JTCC focuses primarily on managing intratheater movements and tasking any transportation assets provided by nations for support of the entire MNF.

(5) NATO's JTMS and JTCC perform similar functions to a US joint movement center (JMC). If the US establishes a separate national JMC for managing movement of US forces in a multinational operation, the JMC must coordinate closely with the multinational movement control centers to ensure synchronized deployment and intratheater movement.

(6) In non-US-led coalitions, the US may be requested to function as LN for deployment planning and movement control because of its expertise in these areas.

d. **Sustain the Force.** Sustainment is the provision of logistics and personnel services required to maintain and prolong operations until successful mission accomplishment. Sustainment is conducted for the duration of the joint mission. A logistic concept of support must complement the overall concept of operations (CONOPS). Logistic planners accomplish this by tailoring the Joint Deployment and Distribution Enterprise (JDDE), including incoming stock, theater excess stock and disposal requirements, or devising new distribution capabilities. The JDDE is that complex system of equipment, procedures, doctrine, leaders, technical connectivity, information, shared knowledge, organizations, facilities, training, and materiel that facilitates the successful conduct of multinational distribution operations.

e. **Staffing.** Multinational movement coordination organizations require a diversity of skilled personnel with expertise in all modes of transportation, including both military and commercial transportation and associated infrastructure. Also required are experts in patient evacuation to coordinate such activities with the medical staff organization. Sustainment organizations require a robust JDDE, which should be tailored to the type of operation being conducted. In non-US-led operations, US JFCs should have staff representation in, or close liaison with, all MNF movement control centers and distribution centers. US MNFCs should work with nations to ensure that they also are represented in similar organizations in US-led operations. MNF liaison with HN forces is crucial in all multinational operations.

f. **Information Requirements.** In order to effectively synchronize and manage multinational movements, the JMC (or equivalent) requires detailed, timely information on individual nation's deployment plans. If possible, information should also be in the format and categories for inclusion in a multinational time-phased force and deployment data (TPFDD) or NATO DDP to support deployment planning and course of action (COA) analysis. For non-US-led operations, US strategic movement planners must have the capability to integrate US deployment data into a non-US deployment planning system, for example, NATO's Allied Deployment and Movement System (ADAMS). The JDDE should have visibility of what levels of stockage are currently in theater and visibility of incoming resupply. Information reporting requirements should be carefully developed and the communications and automated management systems must be readily available to support the JMC and the JDDE (or their equivalents). The information flow includes not only requirements and capabilities but also visibility of movement status. In-transit visibility is essential for tracking the identity, status, and location of assets, from origin to destination, across the range of multinational operations and is critical to managing those assets and delivering them to the required points of application.

See JP 3-35, Deployment and Redeployment Operations, *and JP 4-09,* Distribution Operations, *for additional information.*

5. Health Service Support

a. **Health Service Support.** Nations are ultimately responsible for providing HSS for their forces. Because of national sensitivities, the US strives to rely on national resources for providing HSS to its forces to the maximum extent. Opportunities nevertheless exist to rationalize HSS within a multinational operation. For example, HSS roles of medical care (see JP 4-02, *Health Service Support,* for more information on roles of medical care) could be provided by a LN or role specialist nation (RSN). However, differences in medical standards, customs, and training, require careful consideration in planning multinational medical support. The exchange of blood and blood products between nations is an especially sensitive issue.

More detailed guidance on HSS in multinational operations can be found in JP 4-02, Health Service Support.

(1) The joint force surgeon is responsible for overall planning and coordination of medical support for the MNF. Specific responsibilities include:

(a) Develop overall MNF policy for medical support and promulgate to force participants.

(b) Advise nations in estimating health risk and associated casualties.

(c) Conduct medical assessment of the area.

(d) Develop the operation's overall medical architecture, to include determination of the number, size, capabilities, location, and source of medical facilities.

(e) Review national medical support plans, and integrate into the overall operation HSS plan.

(f) Identify potential use of multinational HSS arrangements and work with nations to develop such arrangements.

(g) Determine the ability of prospective participants to provide medical capabilities for the operation, and assist nations, if requested, in obtaining medical support through multinational assistance.

(h) Establish medical evacuation policy and support concept, and work with nations in rationalizing medical evacuation capabilities through use of LN, RSN, and other multinational arrangements.

(i) Coordinate to ensure adequate blood supply for national contingents, using LN providers, if necessary.

(j) Coordinate planning and execution of treatment of CBRN casualties and MNF requirement for chemoprophylaxis, immunizations, pretreatments, barrier creams, sanitation, first aid, and other requirements in a CBRN environment.

(k) Mass casualty planning.

(2) Because of its robust, high quality medical capabilities, the US may be able to provide HSS to multinational partners, including: Class VIII medical supplies; veterinary services; medical laboratory services; optical fabrication; medical equipment maintenance and repair; preventive medicine; and patient movement (ground and aerial evacuation).

(3) US laws and policies, however, place restrictions on the provision of HSS to other nations and the use of foreign HSS by US forces. US commanders must be aware of such restrictions in non-US-led multinational operations, and inform the MNFC of these restrictions.

(4) A medical coordination cell (MEDCC), in NATO parlance, may be established to work under the technical direction of the force surgeon. The MEDCC (or equivalent) is designed to:

(a) Coordinate multinational, joint, and multifunctional medical issues, including patient evacuation. Coordination of the medical evacuation of casualties from the theater is the most important routine operation of the MEDCC during an operation. The MEDCC coordinates with national elements, the medical facility from which the evacuation will occur, the evacuation providers, and the multinational movement control organization that will coordinate the actual movement of the casualties. Close coordination with appropriate national liaison personnel is extremely critical during this entire process.

(b) Determine the medical capabilities and capacity of prospective participating nations and work with nations to ensure adequate medical support.

(c) Establish medical treatment facilities to assist in the event emergencies exceed an individual nation's capabilities in the operational area.

(d) Determine opportunities to employ LN, RSN, and other multinational arrangements to achieve more efficient and effective use of HSS capabilities within the MNF.

(e) Certify the adequacy of local civil medical/dental resources to meet MNF standards.

(f) Establish veterinary procedures to ensure quality food storage, distribution, and preparation.

(g) Plan and execute a preventive medicine program to reduce nonbattle casualties.

b. **Staffing.** Apart from the administrative and clerical personnel needed to support cell activities, each person should be a skilled health services practitioner. Personnel with expertise in patient evacuation should also be included to work with movement control centers in planning evacuation flights. Ideally, each nation participating in the operation should provide representatives to the MEDCC.

c. **Information Requirements.** The MEDCC depends on critical and timely information regarding, for example, emergency medical requirements and the location of need. A clear picture of the HSS capabilities of participating nations must be developed, shortfalls identified (prior to force deployment), and the need determined for the type of medical facilities required to supplement national or other intratheater medical capabilities. The MEDCC depends on situation reports provided by all elements of the MNF in order to ensure that adequate medical/dental capability is available where and when needed. Of critical importance is the need for an accurate patient tracking system. Medical information connectivity should exist between the MEDCC, national elements, and all members of the medical technical chain.

d. **Coordinating Activities.** The MEDCC coordinates closely with the MNF's movement control center; with the contracting office; with the engineering coordination cell; and with the joint logistics operations center (JLOC) for logistic support. The MEDCC coordinates closely with the host-nation support coordination cell (HNSCC) and civil-military operations center (CMOC) regarding the availability of local civil medical resources to supplement military HSS capabilities.

For details on working with nonmilitary agencies, refer to JP 3-08, Interorganizational Coordination During Joint Operations, *and JP 4-02,* Health Service Support.

6. Engineering

Engineering lends itself to multinational coordination and management arrangements. Nations participating in a multinational operation may place assigned engineer units under the operational control (OPCON) of the engineer task force commander. As alternatives, engineer units may receive tasking from the multinational joint logistic center (MJLC) or equivalent organization, or nations may simply coordinate engineer activities with the MNFC and the force engineer.

a. Engineer operations are a significant force multiplier for the MNFC. MNF engineers integrate, synchronize, and direct engineer operations. These functions include combat engineering, general engineering, and geospatial engineering.

For more information on combat engineering, refer to JP 3-15, Barriers, Obstacles, and Mine Warfare for Joint Operations, *and JP 3-34,* Joint Engineer Operations. *For more information on general engineering support, refer to JP 3-34,* Joint Engineer Operations. *For more information on geospatial engineering, refer to JP 2-03,* Geospatial Intelligence Support to Joint Operations, *and JP 3-34,* Joint Engineer Operations.

b. To assist the force engineer, an engineer coordination element may be established. In a US-led multinational operation, this coordination element will normally comprise a staff element within the logistics directorate of a joint staff and may involve a number of functionally specific joint engineer boards—for example, the joint facilities utilization board (JFUB), joint civil-military engineering board (JCMEB), and joint environmental management board. These joint boards would be expanded with personnel from coalition partners to form combined organizational elements with multinational engineer coordination functions. In NATO doctrine, the central coordinating organization for civil engineering is called an engineer coordination cell (ECC) and may directly support the force engineer, who is a special staff officer under the MNFC. If joint engineer boards have been established in support of US forces in a NATO operation, they should coordinate closely with the ECC. The theater engineer may also establish regional/component subordinate offices to assist the ECC in coordinating multinational engineering activities.

For details on US engineering doctrine, see JP 3-34, Joint Engineer Operations. *For NATO doctrine, see AJP-4,* Allied Joint Logistic Doctrine.

c. Whatever the specific coordinating organization, it is the responsibility of the force engineer (and staff) to effect centralized direction and decentralized execution of the civil engineering effort and to ensure a unified and efficient use of engineering resources for common support of MNF operations. More specifically, it is the responsibility of the force engineer (assisted by the ECC or equivalent) to:

(1) Coordinate with MNFC to determine construction standards for engineering projects (e.g., initial operating capacity versus final operating capacity).

(2) Identify and prioritize requirements for civil engineer projects that support MNF operations.

(3) Work with participating nations to obtain engineer capabilities to execute common engineer projects.

(4) Coordinate with other staff elements or coordination cells (e.g., logistics staff, financial, contracting, and movements control cells) for procurement of engineer materials for both common and national specific engineer projects. Because of the scarcity of engineer materials in some operational areas, it will be necessary to prioritize and centrally coordinate the procurement by nations of engineer material for national and common infrastructure projects.

(5) Coordinate with contracting staff in arranging and prioritizing local engineer capabilities, if available.

(6) Task units provided by nations for common infrastructure projects.

(7) Employ liaison detachments with key participating nations and at critical geographic locations in the operational area to ensure most efficient use of engineer resources.

d. Common funding may be used to fund common infrastructure projects, as it was in NATO peacekeeping operations in Bosnia. The ECC should work with MJLC budget and finance staff in allocating funds for these projects in a timely manner.

e. **Staffing.** Personnel assigned to multinational ECCs should possess appropriate engineering skills and expertise. To the extent possible, appropriate engineer resource specialists should represent each nation involved in the operation and be able to commit their nation's financial resources, monitor the funding process, and oversee execution processes when needed. US contributions to the ECC (or equivalent) may include civilian specialists from Service engineer centers, such as the Air Force Civil Engineer Support Agency. These specialists are most familiar with specialized construction, demolition and other engineering specifications and procedures. The US and other participating nations in multinational operations coordinate with the MNFC in order to ensure that these engineer contractor personnel are appropriately covered in all MNF SOFAs and TAs.

f. **Information Requirements.** The ECC requires standardized project management software (i.e., geospatial/terrain visualization software) that enables the ability to estimate engineer project requirements and costs, monitor project status, and incorporate contractor capabilities to support operational requirements. There is also a need for a reliable communications link with all potential customers to make available clear requirements definitions and funding information.

7. Logistic Services

In addition to MNL coordination centers at the MNF HQ level, nations participating in a multinational operation may determine the need for operational-level support organizations to provide common support for the MNF. Such organizations include naval advanced logistic support sites (NALSSs) and naval forward logistic sites (NFLSs) for supporting multinational maritime forces, and intermediate staging bases (ISBs) for supporting ground and air units. MNL support elements serve as critical transshipment nodes, supply storage and distribution points, refueling stations, staging bases for onward movement into tactical operational zones, medical support centers, and providers of other CUL support. MNL sites may be organized as elements within the MNF C2 structure under the command of the MNFC. Within a NATO maritime operation, for example, NALSSs and NFLSs are elements of the multinational maritime force shore support organization and may report either to a MNL maritime command or directly to a maritime element embedded in the MJLC. In such an organizational structure, NALSSs and NFLSs are multinational organizations with NATO commanders and integrated multinational staff. Multinational support organizations, however, could also be LN-operated organizations that provide support to multinational partners, as requested. For example, the US could establish a national ISB outside the tactical operational area that is used both for staging and supporting US forces and providing logistic services to other nations. In this case, the logistic site providing MNL support is under command of the operating nation (the US), and the site commander coordinates with the MNFC.

a. Logistic services comprise the support capabilities that collectively enable the US to rapidly provide global sustainment for military forces. Logistic services include many disparate activities that are highly scalable capabilities. Included in this area are food, water and ice, base camp, and hygiene services.

For a more complete discussion of joint logistic services, see JP 4-0, Joint Logistics.

b. Mortuary affairs oversight and responsibility currently resides within the multinational staff logistics directorate. Mortuary affairs provides for dignified return of deceased personnel and their personal effects beginning at the mortuary affairs collection point and ending at final disposition.

For a more complete discussion of multinational mortuary affairs operations, see JP 4-06, Mortuary Affairs, *and Department of Defense Directive (DODD) 1300.22E,* Mortuary Affairs Policy.

8. Operational Contract Support

Theater support contracting and CUL-related external theater support contracting make use of regionally available supplies, services, and construction capability in immediate support of deployed units, at staging locations, interim support bases, or forward operating locations. The use of local contractor services can also play a very important role in the economic health within the countries where the operation is being conducted.

a. **Centralized coordination of contracting efforts is essential to provide the necessary management of limited resources to ensure that the MNFC's operational priorities are effectively and efficiently supported.** Through centralized coordination of contracting efforts, maximum benefits are derived from volume procurements, competition is optimized, price escalation is avoided, and the opportunities for local black market operations are minimized. The need to coordinate contracting activities is especially important when locally available supplies and resources may be very limited and the disjointed unilateral competition for such resources could result in bidding up the cost of those services.

b. To most effectively coordinate contracting activities of MNF participants, the MNFC may establish a centralized contracting coordination cell. In NATO doctrine, this organizational element is known as the theater allied contracting office. The contracting coordination office and its regional/component subordinate offices, if established, should develop and maintain close contact with potential contractors, operational customers, other coordination centers (especially the HNSCC), and staff elements such as the command legal counsel and the budget and finance offices.

c. **The establishment of a centralized contracting center is not intended to usurp the contracting prerogatives of any nation.** In multinational operations, commanders of US contracting entities are responsible for contracting operations to support US forces, and contracting officers are guided by US laws and the Federal Acquisition Regulation in obtaining contractor services. The contracting coordination center prioritizes and coordinates national contracting of goods and services that are in limited supply within the operational area or are commonly needed by the entire force (or by more than one component). These commonly needed goods and services may include food, fuel, lodging, labor, construction materials, facilities, and transportation. To effectively coordinate MNF contracting activities, the MNFC may publish a restricted items list that identifies critical, limited supplies and services within the operational area, the procurement of which must be coordinated with the contracting coordination center.

d. In a NATO operation, the theater allied contracting office may also negotiate basic ordering agreements (BOAs) for use by all participating nations, assist nations in negotiating contracts, and negotiate contracts for common-funded MNF activities. In US-led operations, the contracting coordination center, may be an extension of lead Service contracting office or joint theater support contracting command (if established), may be requested to assist nations in similar ways but is likely to focus on coordinating national contracting efforts.

For further guidance on contracting and contractor management, refer to JP 4-0, Joint Logistics, *and JP 4-10,* Operational Contract Support.

e. **Staffing.** Personnel assigned to this center should be skilled in procurement functions. To the extent possible, the personnel should represent each nation involved in the operation and be warranted to commit their nation's financial resources, when needed.

f. **Information Requirements.** A database of goods and services available in the operational area, as well as contractors' capability to support operational requirements, must be developed. There is also a need for a reliable communications link with all potential customers through which a clear definition of requirements and funding information may be made available.

9. National Support Element

An NSE is any national organization or activity that supports national forces that are part of an MNF. NSEs serve as the intermediary between the strategic level of logistic support from nations to their forces at the tactical level. They also coordinate and consolidate CUL functions. Routinely, the US Service component of an MNF which has the preponderance of the lead Service CUL responsibilities would be designated the US NSE responsible to provide CUL support to US forces in a multinational operation. If the US force is geographically dispersed, separate component NSEs might be required. NSEs include nationally commanded NALSSs, NFLSs, ISBs, or other organizations, in the operational area, that support national forces assigned to the MNF.

a. An NSE provides logistic support, including supply, maintenance, transportation, health services, customs and border clearance, engineering, environmental, and contracting and may provide a hedge against enemy interdiction of support capabilities/assets. As noted above, an NSE may provide CUL support to MNFs as well as national forces. It is also possible that in some operations, selected CUL would be arranged by the MJLC (or equivalent), thereby reducing the role of the NSE in providing such logistics.

b. In today's nonlinear operational environment, NSEs are located geographically to best support the force and sited to take advantage of air, rail, and/or sea lines of communications (LOCs). In cases where the MJLC (or equivalent) has real estate management responsibility, nations desiring to locate NSEs in the MNFC's operational area must coordinate with both the MJLC and the HN for final site approval. This is critical in those areas with limited air and sea ports of debarkation (PODs) in which several nations may be competing for limited available space or facilities. NSEs from several nations may be collocated to achieve economies and efficiencies. Some nations may find it especially advantageous to form a combined NSE.

    c. **Command Relationships.** NSEs are national activities that remain under control of national authorities—not the MNFC. There are two basic options for US command relationship of NSEs.

    (1) US NSEs will normally be under direct command of their respective Service component commander.

    (2) In exceptional cases, the US NSE may be a logistically-focused joint task force (JTF) under OPCON to the senior JTF commander.

    (3) Both options are consistent with the practice of most nations, participating in a multinational operation, to designate a national commander in-theater to which the NSE normally reports. In such cases, the national commander retains national control over all national units and other elements not transferred under OPCON of the MNFC.

    d. **Multinational Coordination.** Regardless of the national command relationship that may exist, US NSEs are expected to coordinate and cooperate fully with the appropriate MNF logistic C2 organization, and with the HN. It is incumbent upon the NSEs to provide liaison personnel to such logistic mission control organizations as the MJLC in order to establish and maintain the appropriate relationships.

10. Host-Nation Support

    HNS will often be critical to the success of a multinational operation. Centralized coordination of HNS planning and execution will ensure that limited HNS resources are allocated most effectively to support the MNFC's priorities. The more limited HNS resources are in the operational area, the greater the requirement for centralized management.

    a. In US-led multinational operations, nations typically negotiate their own HNS agreements. Participating nations nevertheless should coordinate their HNS arrangements with the MNFC, who in turn should coordinate HNS allocation with the HN.

    b. To assist the MNFC in HNS coordination activities, an HNSCC may be established. One of the most important functions of the HNSCC is to assist the MNFC and legal counsel in developing TAs that involve logistic matters such as: infrastructure, finance, purchasing and contracting, engineering, environment, hazardous material storage, landing and port fees, medical, border customs, tariffs, and real estate. In US-led multinational operations, the MNFC needs to involve participating nations in the negotiation of either commonly worded separate bilateral TAs or a single set of agreements applicable to the entire MNF.

c. **Staffing.** The HNSCC should be staffed with specialists familiar with developing and executing HNS agreements. In addition, consideration should be given to including representatives of the HN within the HNSCC to:

(1) Facilitate coordination and identification of resources for potential use by the MNF.

(2) Provide interpretation and translation services to the HNSCC staff.

d. **Information Requirements.** In order to effectively plan and coordinate HNS allocation, the HNSCC needs up-to-date information on HNS logistic capabilities and on-going HNS allocation to MNF contingents throughout the operation. To ensure that it receives such information, the HNSCC must maintain close contact with the HN and with MNF contingents. In order to facilitate HNS planning and operational coordination, US GCCs and alliance organizations should develop an HNS catalog or database of potential HNS capabilities in advance of operations.

e. **Coordinating Activities.** In conducting its operations, the HNSCC coordinates closely with appropriate CMOC organizations, the legal, financial, and contracting staff of the MJLC, and the HN's representatives.

f. **Other Logistic Operations**

(1) In addition to the functions discussed above, there are other logistics activities that could benefit from multinational coordination at the theater-level. These activities include:

(a) Petroleum, oils, and lubricants (POL) supply and distribution;

(b) Real estate and environmental management; and

(c) Procurement of fresh rations, water, and ice.

(2) Even services that are normally provided nationally (for example, mortuary affairs) may be amenable to multinational support in some situations. (US doctrine states that in appropriate circumstances, the US may provide mortuary services to multinational partners, or to the local populace in humanitarian operations. See JP 4-06, *Mortuary Affairs*.)

(3) In US-led multinational operations, multinational coordination of these services may be effected through various functional joint boards, cells, and offices, which are expanded to include multinational staff, or through a multinational logistic center (MNLC), or joint logistics coordination center (JLCC) in NATO doctrine. In addition to coordinating specific logistic functions, the MNLC/JLCC provides general oversight of the MNF logistic posture, coordinates all support functions of RSNs and LNs, and exercises tasking authority for assigned operation level logistic units.

g. **Staffing.** The MNLC/JLCC should be staffed with experienced logisticians from participating nations with functional expertise, particularly in supply and maintenance operations, fuels and fuel management, and ration management. The US force commander should consider including representatives from DLA.

h. **Information Requirements.** The MNLC/JLCC is the proponent for gathering logistic information for the MNFC, who are responsible for maintaining visibility of the MNF overall logistic situation. Reporting requirements focus on the critical information required at respective command levels and are included in the logistic support plan. Adequate and timely reporting of information is critical, and US and other national commanders must cooperate in providing such information to the MNFC.

11. Funding and Reimbursement

a. **US Requirements.** In general, nations are expected to fund their participation in MNL support arrangements and reimburse providers for any support received from other nations. Funding and reimbursement requirements for US participation in these arrangements are generally a function of the applicable US legal authority. For example, US support provided under an LN/RSN or emergency support arrangement is generally implemented under the Arms Export Control Act (AECA) or ACSA authority, respectively. In these cases, funding and reimbursement are managed in accordance with the funding procedures for these authorities. However, some multinational support arrangements, such as provision of national logistic assets to a MNL organization or participation in a multinational integrated logistic unit (MILU), may involve deferral or waiver of reimbursement. US CCDRs who envision participating in support arrangements for which reimbursement is to be waived should receive approval from higher HQ. A decision to waive or defer reimbursement for support provided to other nations is ultimately a political decision and is transmitted from the President and Secretary of Defense through the Chairman of the Joint Chiefs of Staff (CJCS), to the commander.

Detailed policies and procedures for funding and reimbursement in multinational logistic operations are described in JP 1-06, Financial Management Support in Joint Operations.

b. **Financial Reporting.** US participation in MNL operations requires regular financial reporting. The content and source of these reports vary with the controlling legal authority. In general, the Defense Finance and Accounting Service, in coordination with the security assistance offices of the responsible Military Department, prepares and distributes financial and other reports on support provided under the AECA and Section 506 of the Foreign Assistance Act (FAA). GCCs should ensure that they receive copies of these reports. The responsible geographic combatant command Service component prepares reports on support provided under an ACSA and forwards them to the GCC and Military Department as input for an annual report to Congress. Service component commanders are also responsible for ensuring that their allocated ceiling on the value of ACSA acquisition and exchanges is not exceeded. The GCC is responsible for allocating to each Service component its share of the statutory ceiling on ACSA activity. The responsible Service component commander prepares reports on support provided under Section 607 of the FAA and forwards them to appropriate CCDRs when requested. Failure to complete these reports will result in failure to recoup the costs of providing the support.

    c. **Common Funding.** Common funding—national funds paid into a common account managed by an alliance organization (e.g., NATO) or an IGO (e.g., the UN)—can be an invaluable means of funding common logistic requirements essential to the start of an operation. Common funding can also reduce the necessity for the US to unilaterally fund those requirements. Examples of common-funded items include international HQ operating expenses, common communication systems, and improvements to theater supply routes and airfields. US commanders assigned as MNFCs need to identify potential requirements, sources, and procedures for obtaining common funding as early as possible. In situations where pre-established common funds are not available or do not cover all relevant areas, other funding arrangements must be developed ad hoc. The methodology for sharing common costs must also be determined in cases where two or more nations form MILUs, integrated operational units, or support groups (e.g., multinational NSEs). Contributions to a common fund must be based on a mutually agreed-upon formula as well as the basis for allocating operational costs.

CHAPTER III
MULTINATIONAL LOGISTIC PLANNING

"Logistics comprises the means and arrangements which work out the plans of strategy and tactics. Strategy decides where to act; logistics brings the troops to this point."

Antoine-Henri baron de Jomini,
***Précis de l'Art de la Guerre*, 1838**

1. Introduction

This chapter provides guidance to US MNFCs and their staffs in the development of MNL support plans. This guidance is intended to complement doctrine and procedures developed by alliances and IGOs that have been ratified by the US, and to serve as the basis for planning logistic support in operations where such guidance does not apply. This chapter also provides guidance for developing logistic support plans for US forces participating in multinational operations and for selected transition operations involving US and MNFs. Centralized coordinated planning is required to ensure smooth MNF deployment. The allocation of HNS and operational contract support reduces logistic footprints. Logistic planning of multinational operations poses considerable challenges. Realistically, only a few nations can logistically support themselves in every operational phase: deployment; sustainment; and redeployment/termination.

a. MNL planning is complicated by several factors:

(1) Advance planning for multinational operations is usually confined only to close allies that are highly likely to join with the US in the planned operation. Even among close allies, some PNs may be reluctant to support advance planning of US involved operations. As a result, most planning for multinational operations, therefore, tends to be ad hoc.

(2) Nations are generally reluctant in the early planning process to commit forces to the MNF. This is especially true regarding logistic contributions to MNF support. Logistic planning for multinational operations, therefore, can be a lengthy iterative process during which nations come to agreement on the logistic C2 organization and support arrangements only after extensive deliberation.

(3) Given these factors, planning for multinational operations usually commences only after the crisis has developed. Since logistics often is a limiting factor in operations, logistic planning needs to be initiated as soon as possible and occur concurrently with operational planning.

(4) Within a multinational operation it is imperative that participating nations have confidence in the way partners are supporting their forces. Nations are often reluctant to, and sometimes prohibited from, sharing national OPLANs with potential partners because of national security. Nonetheless, efforts should be made to share operation and logistic support plans during the plan development stage. While selected details may not be shared,

general logistic support concepts, possible force/resource contributions, logistic support requirements, capabilities, and possible support arrangements should be discussed.

(5) An information database regarding the logistic capabilities of potential multinational partners is crucial for effective MNL planning. During peacetime, US and multinational planners may be able to use such information to identify—in advance—possible MNL contributions to an operation and to implement programs, including multinational exercises and planning seminars, to enhance interoperability. United States Pacific Command's Multinational Planning Augmentation Team program is a good example that enhances MNL planning and provides planners with the requisite planning tools.

b. To more effectively integrate partners in contingency logistics planning, the MNFC should consider the following measures:

(1) Seek early assignment of logistic planners from participating nations to the MNFC logistic planning staff.

(2) Produce MNL planning templates using US/LN data and planning factors. Templates would be filled out by participating nation logistic planners.

(3) Arrange temporary assignment of US/LN logistic liaison officers to the national HQ of participating nations.

(4) Provide access to US/LN logistic information management systems or arrange electronic interface between compatible national systems where feasible.

(5) Seek early briefings on participating nation logistic capabilities and shortfalls and obtain commitments to cooperative logistic arrangements.

(6) Seek early staffing for MJLC (or equivalent) functional coordination bodies.

c. National operational preferences influence the degree to which nations are willing to rely on MNL during the early phase(s) of an operation. Nevertheless, early MNL planning increases the options available to national commanders for employing MNL for mutual benefit during the critical first stages of an operation.

2. Planning

a. **Perspective of US MNFC.** When functioning as the MNFC, US commanders have the responsibility to develop a CONOPS and initial concept of support, in coordination with participating nations. Upon approval of participating nations, US and other MNL planners iteratively develop the support plan during a series of planning conferences, as time allows. US MNFCs should address the following critical logistic issues in planning for multinational operations.

(1) Logistic C2 relationships and organizational structure. Given differences in national terminology, it is essential that participating nations operate with the same understanding of C2 relationships.

(2) Structure, staffing, and equipment of MNL organizations. Personnel from participating nations need to be integrated into MNF logistic HQ organizations to make them truly multinational.

(3) Logistic authorities and responsibilities of the MNFC and participating nations.

(4) Logistic reporting requirements and reporting capabilities of participating nations.

(5) Interoperability of logistic C2, communications, and information systems within the force. Achieving interoperable logistic C2, communications, and intelligence is difficult, even with long-time allies. To facilitate C2, communications, and intelligence interoperability, the US commander serving as an MNFC may need to provide requisite systems to multinational partners.

(6) Logistic requirements for national contingents (e.g., level of medical support, amount of supplies to be maintained in the operational area).

(7) Logistic capabilities of participating national contingents. The MNFC needs to know to what extent national contingents may require support from nonorganic resources in order to develop a logistic plan for the operation. NATO doctrine currently requires certification of the logistic capabilities of non-NATO contingents before they participate in non-Article 5 crisis response operations. Similar "certifications" may not be relevant or required for US-led coalitions and, in any case, may be beyond the resources of the US MNFC and staff to conduct. However, even in the case of less formal logistic assessments, the US commander serving as an MNFC should be aware that such assessments of multinational partner capabilities may be diplomatically or politically sensitive and require multinational cooperation.

(8) Requirements for force-wide mutual support arrangements and implementing mechanisms.

(9) Requirements for multinational support, including requirements for theater/operational-level logistic forces.

(10) Concepts for logistic functions and use of MNL support arrangements, such as RSN and LN, to implement such concepts.

(11) Prioritized requirements for HNS and theater support contracting resources.

(12) Authorities and responsibilities of the MNFC and nations in arranging support from host and transited nations. Centralized coordination of intratheater resource allocation is essential for operationally efficient support of multinational operations.

(13) Availability of logistic planning tools, including logistic intelligence databases in the operational area, and responsibilities for developing and maintaining such databases.

(14) Differences in classes of supply, see Figure III-1.

UNITED STATES AND NORTH ATLANTIC TREATY ORGANIZATION CLASSES OF SUPPLY		
Class of Supply	US	North Atlantic Treaty Organization
I	Subsistence--rations and gratuitous issue of health, morale, and welfare items.	Personal consumption items.
II	Clothing, individual equipment, tentage, tool sets, and administrative and housekeeping supplies and equipment.	Items established by tables of organization and equipment (TOE)--e.g., clothing, weapons, tools, spare parts, vehicles.
III	Petroleum, oils, and lubricants.	Fuel and lubricants, except aircraft and weapons fuel.
IIIa		Aviation fuel and lubricants.
IV	Construction materials.	Non-TOE items, such as fortification and construction materials and additional vehicles.
V	Ammunition.	Ammunition, explosives, and chemical agents of all types.
VI	Personal demand items.	
VII	Major end items--includes tanks, helicopters, and radios.	
VIII	Medical.	
IX	Repair parts and components for equipment maintenance.	
X	Nonstandard items to support nonmilitary programs such as agriculture and economic development.	

Figure III-1. United States and North Atlantic Treaty Organization Classes of Supply

(15) Mechanisms to protect logistic technical databases and logistic information systems.

(16) Relationships with and support to IGOs, NGOs, and other nonmilitary organizations.

(17) Coordination with US non-DOD departments and agencies on logistic matters affecting the mission/operation. In addition to normal United States Government (USG) interagency coordination efforts and procedures, CCDRs can use their joint interagency coordination group and the associated or attached USG department or agency representatives and command liaison officers to facilitate and foster logistics planning and coordination.

(18) Applicability of existing NATO or ABCA standardization agreements to serve as a basis for quick development of standardized coalition logistic procedures.

(19) Requirements for infrastructure improvements within the operational area and funding arrangements for such improvements.

(20) Logistic-related items, such as landing rights, customs, taxes, and environmental issues, to be addressed in SOFAs and supporting TAs.

(21) Environmental considerations and hazardous material/waste treatment and removal.

(22) Up-front common funding authority and availability of funds.

(23) FP measures for logistic sites and activities.

(24) In addressing these issues, US MNFCs should keep in mind cultural aspects of multinational partners that could affect the operation (e.g., dietary preferences, physical characteristics, and religious practices and taboos).

Appendix A provides a "Commander's Checklist for Logistics in Support of Multinational Operations."

b. **US Commander's Perspective.** The US commander should be an early and active participant in the planning process, anticipate support requests, identify US support requirements, and be prepared to respond appropriately. Close and continuous coordination with the Joint Staff may also be necessary, especially when Secretary of Defense approval is required for US participation in a specific MNL support arrangement—for example, acceptance of RSN or LN responsibility. In cases where the US force commander is not "dual-hatted" as the MNFC, the following critical planning tasks should be addressed:

(1) Incorporate MNFC logistic guidance into US support plans.

(2) Coordinate US logistic planning with MNFC logistic planning and maintain continuous liaison.

(3) Determine sources of support from the HN and theater support contractors and consult with other participating nations and the MNFC in identifying potential multinational support arrangements. (The US must clearly identify the extent to which it can participate in multinational support arrangements.)

(4) Notify the MNFC as to the logistic supplies and services that the US will make available to support other participants in the MNF and what limits there are on such support. (US logistic contributions to the MNF are approved by the Secretary of Defense and communicated to MNFC planning staffs.)

(5) If additional ACSA agreements are required, coordinate with designated negotiating authorities (generally the cognizant GCC) and ensure that Service components identify points of contact and implementation procedures for this authority.

(6) Notify the MNFC regarding what logistic assets are available for possible redistribution.

(7) Notify the MNFC of relevant aspects of the US support plan in order to assist the MNFC in harmonizing support for the entire MNF.

(8) Coordinate with nations contributing forces to US units (divisions, brigades, air wings, maritime task forces) regarding support available from the framework unit and on what terms.

(9) Promulgate MNFC logistics policy, plans, and procedures to participating US units.

(10) Assemble databases from all available sources on logistic capabilities of non-US units operating within US framework units and with nations, including HNs, located in the operational area.

(11) Determine FP requirements for US logistic forces, coordinate measures with the MNFC and HNs, and obtain clear specification of responsibilities of US forces, HNs, and other multinational participants.

(12) Review US legal authorities and notify the MNFC regarding any legal constraints that might have an impact on US participation in MNL activities.

(13) Reference lessons learned information systems during the planning process.

Appendix A, "Commander's Checklist for Logistics in Support of Multinational Operations," and Appendix B, "Alternative Formats for Logistics Annex to Multinational Operation Plan," are provided to assist US commanders and logistic staffs prepare to participate in multinational operations.

c. To address significant activities such as predeployment planning, deployment, sustainment, and redeployment/termination the text below provides notional examples of potential activities to be accomplished during a campaign or major operation.

(1) **Predeployment Planning.** MNL planning is critical **prior to the deployment** of the MNF. At the CCDR level, the operations directorate of a joint staff identifies the national caveats for employment of the specific MNFs prior to deployment. This generates the essential equipment and sustainment requirements for the MNF. Logistics planners then engage in identifying potential logistic shortfalls (requires integrated, multinational staff effort) and pursue meeting sustainment requirements. A lack of MNL support planning during predeployment will make logistics planners at all levels reactive to sustainment shortfalls of the MNF and could result in decreased operational flexibility for MNF employment within the theater of operations.

(2) **Deployment** includes strategic movement from ports of embarkation (POEs) to PODs in the operational area and RSOI.

(a) Figure III-2 lists key MNFC activities that should be addressed during the deployment planning phase. In the case of a US-led multinational operation, the MNFC works with nations in developing DDPs in formats that can be incorporated into a single time-phased force and deployment list (TPFDL). MNFC organizations involved in synchronizing the flow of forces are kept up-to-date on conditions in the operational area that could disrupt force deployment. The MNFC should be kept informed on any changes in national deployment plans. To the extent that such changes impact on the MNFC's CONOPS, alternative COAs are developed for the commander's approval. The resultant changes are then immediately communicated to all deploying forces.

(b) The US commander should perform the following in planning deployment of US forces in a multinational operation.

Key Multinational Force Commander Tasks
During Deployment Planning

- Assign final destination, required delivery dates, ports of debarkation (PODs), and deployment routes to deploying formations, based on the commander's operational plan.

- Provide guidance to participating nations regarding modes of transportation and transportation assets.

- Harmonize individual national detailed deployment plans into a single integrated multinational deployment plan.

- Define the command and control organization to manage, coordinate, and control force deployment.

- Identify the number and type of logisticians (especially contracting and budget/finance personnel) to be included as part of the enabling force.

- Arrange host-nation support (HNS) for port reception of deploying forces or arrange for lead nation/role specialist nation operation of PODs.

- Arrange for use of host-nation transportation infrastructure.

- Arrange HNS for onward movement, or arrange contributions from troop-sending nations of transportation/cargo handling assets to support onward movement.

- Identify logistic requirements for support of deploying forces, including emergency medical support, vehicle recovery, engineering, and troop support.

- Arrange for such support from the host nation or theater support contractors.

Figure III-2. Key Multinational Force Commander Tasks During Deployment Planning

1. Develop a DDP for US forces and coordinate with the MNFC in harmonizing the plan with other national deployment plans.

2. Establish connectivity between US and MNFC deployment planning systems, e.g., the Joint Operation Planning and Execution System and ADAMS.

3. Identify requirements for reception and onward movement and coordinate with the MNFC and participating nations in planning multinational arrangements for the most operationally efficient provision of such support.

4. Identify US logistic capabilities that are available to support deploying forces, if requested.

<u>5.</u> Ensure FP of deploying US forces, including civilian contractor personnel accompanying the force.

(3) **Sustainment Operations.** In planning for sustainment, both US MNFCs and national commanders face a common challenge—how to be responsive in providing logistic support to mission forces while minimizing the logistic footprint in the operational area. Both the MNFC and US force commanders should plan for maximum feasible use of multinational arrangements to achieve both objectives.

(a) The key tasks to be accomplished by US and other MNFCs during planning for this phase are shown in Figure III-3. Planning by the MNFC for the sustainment phase requires a thorough understanding of the logistic support requirements and capabilities of participating nations. As part of this process, a methodology should be adopted for determining the ability of each nation to support its forces (whether through organic resources or other means). The MNFC (US or other nationality) needs to build trust and confidence with coalition MNF so that they will cooperate in this effort.

(b) In planning for sustainment of US forces during a multinational operation, US commanders should:

Key Multinational Force Commander Tasks
During Sustainment Planning

- Identify critical sustainment requirements for the operation.

- Develop concepts of support, including multinational force commander (MNFC) and national responsibilities for sustainment functions.

- Prioritize requirements for host-nation support and arrange such support on behalf of participating nations.

- Identify candidate logistic functions for lead nation or role specialist nation assignment and solicit candidate nations.

- Establish policy for theater support contracting in the operational area and identify restricted items requiring MNFC purchasing approval.

- Identify requirements for common funding.

- Establish requirements for logistic reporting and specify reporting formats.

- Identify requirements for staffing multinational logistic organizations.

- Develop environmental policy and procedures for preventing environmental damage and managing environmental restoration.

Figure III-3. Key Multinational Force Commander Tasks During Sustainment Planning

<u>1</u>. Cooperate with the MNFC and other participating nations to take full advantage of opportunities for MNL in sustaining US forces.

<u>2</u>. Coordinate with the MNFC in harmonizing US sustainment planning with multinational planning.

<u>3</u>. Develop concepts for providing support to non-US elements assigned to US framework units and ensure available resources for multinational support.

<u>4</u>. Establish communications links for reporting logistic status of forces to the MNFC, as required.

<u>5</u>. Make provisions for possible emergency support of other participating forces and multinational HQ and ensure enabling authorities are available.

(4) **Redeployment/Termination**

(a) **Redeployment.** In many respects, redeployment of forces from a multinational operation is similar to the deployment process, and therefore in planning redeployment, the MNFC and nations must address many of the same requirements as in deployment. Redeployment, however, may pose additional planning requirements that the MNFC and nations need to collectively address. Figure III-4 lists key MNFC activities that should be addressed during the redeployment/termination planning phase.

Key Multinational Force Commander Tasks During Redeployment/Termination Planning

- Identify requirements for port improvements to support redeployment.

- Coordinate/arrange multinational support for cleaning vehicles to meet national agricultural standards.

- Assist nations in coordinating environmental restoration efforts.

- Account for property of multinational headquarters and determine plan for property disposal.

- Coordinate with host nation regarding return of borrowed equipment and real estate.

- Prepare guidance on disposal of common funded equipment and multinational force property disposal activities.

- Cross-border clearance requirements.

- Nation-specific movement regulations.

Figure III-4. Key Multinational Force Commander Tasks During Redeployment/Termination Planning

---

For detailed information and guidance on redeployment, see JP 3-35, Deployment and Redeployment Operations.

(b) **Termination.** The MNFC and nations collectively plan logistic activities relating to operation termination. A time-phased termination plan should be developed to address the following logistics transition issues:

<u>1.</u> **Property Accounting.** For the multinational HQ, property must be accounted for and decisions made as to the disposition of excess property. Borrowed real estate or facilities must be returned to the host or owning nation.

<u>2.</u> **Environmental Matters.** The MNFC implements guidance to conduct redeployment operations consistent with applicable laws, regulations, and agreements relating to environmental remediation. Under US law, regulation, and policy, the use of appropriated funds for such remediation is prohibited unless specifically authorized. Absent existing authority, it may be necessary for a US MNFC to obtain authority to negotiate and conclude an appropriate agreement.

<u>3.</u> **Equipment Disposal.** Participating countries may decide to dispose of property and equipment in the operational area. Borrowed equipment must be returned to the host or owning nation. The MNFC issues guidance on the disposal of common-funded equipment. In addition, the MNFC issues guidance on property disposal activities by participating nations.

CHAPTER IV
EXECUTING MULTINATIONAL LOGISTICS

> *"We should expect to participate in a broad range of deterrent, conflict prevention, and peacetime activities. Further, our history, strategy, and recent experience suggest that we will usually work in concert with our friends and allies in almost all operations."*
>
> **Harry S. Truman (1884-1972)**

1. Introduction

Although MNF support requirements are similar to those of a joint force, the execution of MNL operations has special considerations necessary for unity of effort. Differences in military organization, security procedures, language, doctrine, and equipment can pose potential risks to the successful implementation of the operations. The risks can be mitigated through adhering to the MNF chain of command, the use of liaisons, and the establishment of a central node for MNL coordination.

2. Multinational Logistics Execution

a. Forces participating in multinational operations have two distinct chains of command: a national chain of command and a multinational chain of command. Effective execution of logistics in MNF operations is contingent upon implementing the OPLAN and understanding the degree of authority that the supported commander has; understanding the responsibilities of the supporting commander; understanding national agreements and arrangements; and understanding the roles and responsibilities of multinational partners. Adhering to the command authority that is negotiated between the participating nations during execution is essential in order to deconflict competition for limited resources, infrastructure, and to facilitate achieving unity of effort in MNF operations. Executing cooperative logistics in multinational operations is conducted using the LN method, pooled assets and resources method, or the role specialization agreement method. The methods to be used are established in the planning process and executed either singularly or in combination.

For additional information on command relationships, see JP 3-16, Multinational Operations.

b. Liaisons and interpreters enable effective integration and synchronization of available assets during MNF operation. Using a liaison network is a significant source of information for the MNFC. Liaisons provide knowledge in the differences in doctrine, organization, equipment, training, and national law demand for PNs. Best practice in execution of multinational operations reveals that the early establishment of a liaison network with forces of each nation, fosters better understanding of missions, tactics, and logistics security operations; facilitates the ability to integrate and synchronize operations; assists in the transfer of vital information during operations; enhances mutual trust; and develops an increased level of teamwork necessary for mission accomplishment. Liaison elements should have appropriate communication linguistic, logistic, and office support capabilities in place to facilitate execution during MNF operations.

For additional information on liaison operations see JP 4-0, Joint Logistics, and JP 3-16, Multinational Operations. For additional information on logistics security see JP 4-09, Distribution Operations.

    c. Multinational coordination centers can be used to integrate PNs into the execution of MNF operations. Coordination centers (referred to as centers for this discussion) can be in the form of MNL boards, cells, centers, groups, offices, or teams. Coordination centers should be established as early as possible and be used extensively during execution in order to facilitate unified action. PNs should establish MNF coordination center(s) (for parallel command structure) or integrated HQ staff (for integrated command structure or LN command structure). Centers and staffs facilitate activities including personnel movement, medical support, ground and air evacuation, contracting, infrastructure engineering, and logistic operations. Using coordination centers during execution aids in the deconfliction and maximization of the fulfillment of transportation requirements, control of contract personnel, exchange of mutual logistic support of goods and services, as well as determining which element in the MNF provides which pieces of the logistics system, health services, and logistics reporting. Additionally, coordination centers facilitate the rationalization, standardization, and interoperability needed during execution of MNF operations.

For additional information on coordination centers, see JP 4-0, Joint Logistics, and JP 3-16, Multinational Operations.

3. Transitioning to a Multinational Operation

    a. **Transitioning from a US Joint Operation to a Multinational Operation.** The US may find it necessary to initiate military action before an international consensus develops (such as Operation RESTORE HOPE in Somalia). Following the development of international support, a multinational operation, conducted by an alliance or a coalition, possibly under UN or NATO management, may be authorized.

    (1) Since the US may have an extensive logistic structure already in place in the operational area, it may be asked to assume the lead role in the MNL organization—at least for a transition period. The senior US logistic commander may be designated as the senior logistics commander for the MNF and be given specified authorities and responsibilities by the MNFC. Additionally, US contracts and HNS agreements may become the vehicles for multinational agreements. The US may also be asked to assume LN and RSN roles. LN and RSN roles may require the use of a logistics civil augmentation program (LOGCAP); Air Force contract augmentation program (AFCAP); and construction capabilities contract program contractors, Naval Facilities Engineering Command (NAVFAC) contingency construction, and service contracts for supporting the MNF.

(2) The extent to which the US accepts logistic responsibilities for the MNF is decided by the Secretary of Defense. However, two conditions are critical for a smooth transition to multinational support:

(a) The US should have the proper legal arrangements (e.g., ACSAs) in place to provide logistic support to members of the deploying MNF.

(b) PNs should be prepared to reimburse the US for logistic services rendered, unless other arrangements have been made.

b. **Transitioning from a UN Operation to a Multinational Operation**

(1) In transitioning from a UN operation to another multinational operation, as in the transition from the United Nations Protection Force (UNPROFOR) to NATO's Implementation Force in Bosnia, the UN may remain the lead agency for humanitarian assistance within the operational area. In this case, the MNFC should be prepared to consider requests for assistance from IGOs and NGOs in accomplishing their humanitarian mission. A UN representative HQ organization should remain in the area and serve as the coordinating point of contact for possible assistance requests.

(2) The incoming MNFC should use the intratheater UN infrastructure and organizations to facilitate early development and establishment of the new MNF.

(3) Essential to the successful transition is the development of a cooperative environment between UN and the new MNF. If a UN force or HQ is withdrawing from the operational area, the new MNF should negotiate the transfer of materiel and infrastructure/facilities with the UN commander as appropriate. This procedure would apply in reverse should a UN force relieve another MNF. In addition, agreements between the UN and the MNF are necessary to coordinate the shared use of specified resources. Claims relating to incidents occurring prior to the MNF assuming command of operations are the responsibility of the UN.

(4) To effect a smooth transition, working groups should be established at the appropriate levels to coordinate administrative, financial, and logistic matters.

(5) A critical component of the transition is the reorganization, certification, and reflagging of possible UN units, including logistic forces, to the MNFC.

(6) In the past, the US, as a member of an alliance or coalition, has been called upon to plan for extracting UN peacekeeping forces from threatening situations, as was the case with UNPROFOR in the Balkans. In this kind of operation, normal logistic support for threatened UN forces would likely be disrupted and the US might be required to support UN contingents during extraction operations.

c. **Reduction of US Force Commitment in a Multinational Operation**

(1) In supporting US national interests and contingency operations, JFCs may need to withdraw some or all of their forces from a multinational operation in order to execute

other missions. US forces participating in a multinational operation must maintain sufficient flexibility in MNL arrangements, to the extent warranted by the Secretary of Defense risk assessments, to be able to logistically disengage from the operation and to support redeployment to another operational area. MNFCs may also need to adapt their logistic plans to accommodate possible changes in US force contributions.

(2) On the other hand, the US requirement for MNL arrangements may increase as the size of the US force contribution in an operation decreases. The same principle applies to the entire MNF, especially in peacekeeping operations, as the operation progresses and the total size of the force is reduced.

CHAPTER V
COMMAND AND CONTROL

"The joint force of 2020 must be prepared to "win" across the full range of military operations in any part of the world, to operate with multinational forces, and to coordinate military operations, as necessary, with government agencies and international organizations...Mutual support relationships and collaborative planning will enable optimum cooperation with multinational and interagency partners."

Joint Vision 2020

1. Introduction

The C2 structure for managing logistics during a multinational operation includes the authorities and responsibilities exercised by the MNFC and nations and the C2 through which the MNFC and nations exercise their assigned authorities and responsibilities. The logistic C2 structure established for a multinational operation should complement and be integral to the operation's overall C2 structure. There is no single logistic C2 arrangement that best fits the needs of all multinational operations. Although the specific structure will vary from operation to operation, any MNL C2 structure will typically reflect the considerations highlighted in this chapter.

a. A flexible MNF C2 structure needs to be established early in the planning cycle to coordinate national and MNL operations and support the MNFC's CONOPS. It should include coordinating mechanisms and procedures to facilitate linkages with the appropriate operational HQ, senior coordinating agencies/HQ, component commands, and other national HQ, as appropriate. The MNFC's authority for logistic matters should be clearly defined in the OPLAN.

b. MNF C2 activities should be organized on the basis of the operational mission and coordinated with nations to obtain support and manning for the structure. In alliances, the MNL C2 structure normally is established in peacetime in order to improve contingency planning, participate in exercises, establish manning requirements for actual operations, and serve as an integral component of the operational planning process. For coalition operations, the MNL C2 structure may not be established in advance.

c. In anticipation of participating in multinational operations, GCCs should establish the capability to coordinate future MNL operations within existing US JTF planning structures/HQ to facilitate expansion during multinational operations. Effort should be made to minimize the potentially adverse impact of last minute, ad hoc MNL support arrangements.

d. MNL C2 operations require the use of an effective liaison system, consisting of technically skilled logistic representatives. In order to gain full benefits from MNL arrangements, US commanders must be familiar with the logistic procedures of the MNF, whether NATO, UN, LN as well as the HN. Effective MNL support requires that the MNFC develop a spirit of cooperation, coordination, and communication with and among participating nations.

e. The MNL C2 structure, therefore, should be tailored to each particular operation and will be based on several factors:

(1) Type of operation.

(2) Size of operational area.

(3) Number of participating nations.

(4) Political interests and culture of the participating nations.

(5) Number of components involved.

(6) Extent of HNS and theater contractor support available.

(7) Complexity of the operation.

2. Authorities and Responsibilities

JP 1, *Doctrine for the Armed Forces of the United States*, describes the four levels of command authority available to US commanders: combatant command (command authority) (COCOM), OPCON, tactical control (TACON), and support. Other authorities outside the command relations include administrative control, coordinating authority, and direct liaison authorized. JP 3-16, *Multinational Operations*, describes the general use of these authorities in multinational operations. Each of these levels of authority except COCOM—may apply to US logistic forces assigned to a multinational operation.

a. Operational Control

(1) In multinational operations, the US and other participating nations continue to exercise command over their forces throughout the operation. Generally, however, nations give the MNFC OPCON over their assigned forces (with qualifications discussed in JP 3-16, *Multinational Operations,* for placing US forces under OPCON of UN commanders). The MNFC must be aware that many different interpretations of OPCON and TACON exist among alliance and multinational partners and must ensure complete understanding of the terms early in the planning of the operation. The fundamental elements of US command apply when US forces are placed under the OPCON of a foreign commander.

(2) One element of OPCON, which is also shared by NATO, is that OPCON of itself does not include authority over administrative and logistic functions. Thus, in granting OPCON of US forces to the MNFC, the degree of MNFC coordination and tasking over administrative and logistic functions must be specified.

(3) In addition, the MNFC may be given authority to exercise TACON of ground units transiting through the joint security area. This consideration may apply regardless of whether the operational area resembles the traditional linear or nonlinear operational area.

See JP 3-10, Joint Security Operations in Theater, *for additional information.*

b. Coordination Authority

(1) Typically, the US and other nations will grant the MNFC coordinating authority over common logistic matters during a multinational operation. Under coordinating authority, the MNFC can require consultation between forces but does not have the authority to compel agreement. Coordinating authority recognizes the consultation relationship necessary for forces of sovereign nations to reach consensus during multinational operations to achieve the objective. The US MNFC, when also assigned as the US forces commander, is delegated directive authority for common support capabilities for US forces. Other nations participating in the MNF, however, may only grant the US MNFC coordinating authority over national logistic activities in the operational area.

(2) In addition to granting the MNFC coordinating authority, the US and other participating nations may place logistic units under the OPCON of the MNFC for tasking in support of the MNF.

c. Other Authorities

(1) The US may also grant the MNFC the authority to redistribute logistic resources to meet exigent requirements during an operation. For example, MC 319/2, *NATO Principles and Policies for Logistics,* gives NATO commanders the authority to "direct the redistribution of national logistic resources to overcome unanticipated deficiencies." There are strict restrictions, however, on what assets can be redistributed and under what circumstances and nations have the right to withhold specific logistic resources from redistribution.

(2) The US and other participating nations may grant MNFCs directive authority for common support capabilities in other areas consistent with the OPCON of assigned and attached combat forces. Such authority, however, may only be granted to the MNFC through prearranged agreements.

(3) Normally, tanker airlift control elements and aircrews under the COCOM of the Commander, USTRANSCOM either transiting or based in the operational area are excluded from MNFC exercise of control.

(4) Because C2 relationships within a multinational operation differ significantly from single nation operations, and nations may understand key terms differently, it is important that participating nations clearly understand the extent of the MNFC's logistic authorities and responsibilities—and their limitations—during each operation.

For details regarding C2 in the rear area, see JP 3-10, Joint Security Operations in Theater.

3. Control and Coordination Models

a. Logistic C2 Organizations

(1) The logistic C2 organization of a multinational operation encompasses both the internal logistic staff elements of the MNF HQ and the overall logistic organization, as integrated into the total MNF C2 structure.

(2) If the operation is relatively small or involves only a few multinational partners, the MNFC may rely on the combined-joint logistics officer (CJ-4) and staff, augmented (if necessary) with functional experts, to plan and coordinate MNF logistic activities.

(3) In the case of larger, more complex operations requiring more coordination and common support, the MNFC may establish a separate organization to assist the CJ-4 in developing and executing the operation's logistic support plan. NATO designates such an organization for coordinating and managing MNF logistics such as a MJLC.

(4) For a US-led multinational operation, the JFC may establish an organization functionally-similar to the MJLC that is tailored in size and specific functions to the particular operation. This organization may be designated combined/joint logistics center, MNL coordination center, or the like.

(5) The MJLC (or its equivalent), if established, may be established as:

(a) An augmentation to the CJ-4's staff, especially during initial planning or for smaller operations of limited duration.

(b) A separate staff section within the CJ-4 organization.

(c) A separate organization integrated in or colocated with the MN HQ or other supporting HQ.

(d) A module placed within a component command.

(6) As shown in Figure V-1, the MJLC may consist of various functional coordination centers (or other equivalent bodies) that provide centralized coordination of common support services, such as engineering, movement control, medical activities, contracting, HNS, and the provision of common supplies, such as bulk fuel and rations. The terminology used to designate such organizations and their specific functions varies depending on the command organization for the operation (e.g., NATO, US-led coalition, ABCA coalition).

(7) In a US-led multinational operation, for example, the MJLC could comprise a number of joint logistic centers, offices, and boards that would be expanded to include coordination of MNL matters. These bodies could include combined versions of a: joint logistics readiness center or JLOC, JMC, joint petroleum office, JCMEB, JFUB, CCDR logistics procurement support board, theater patient movement requirements center, joint

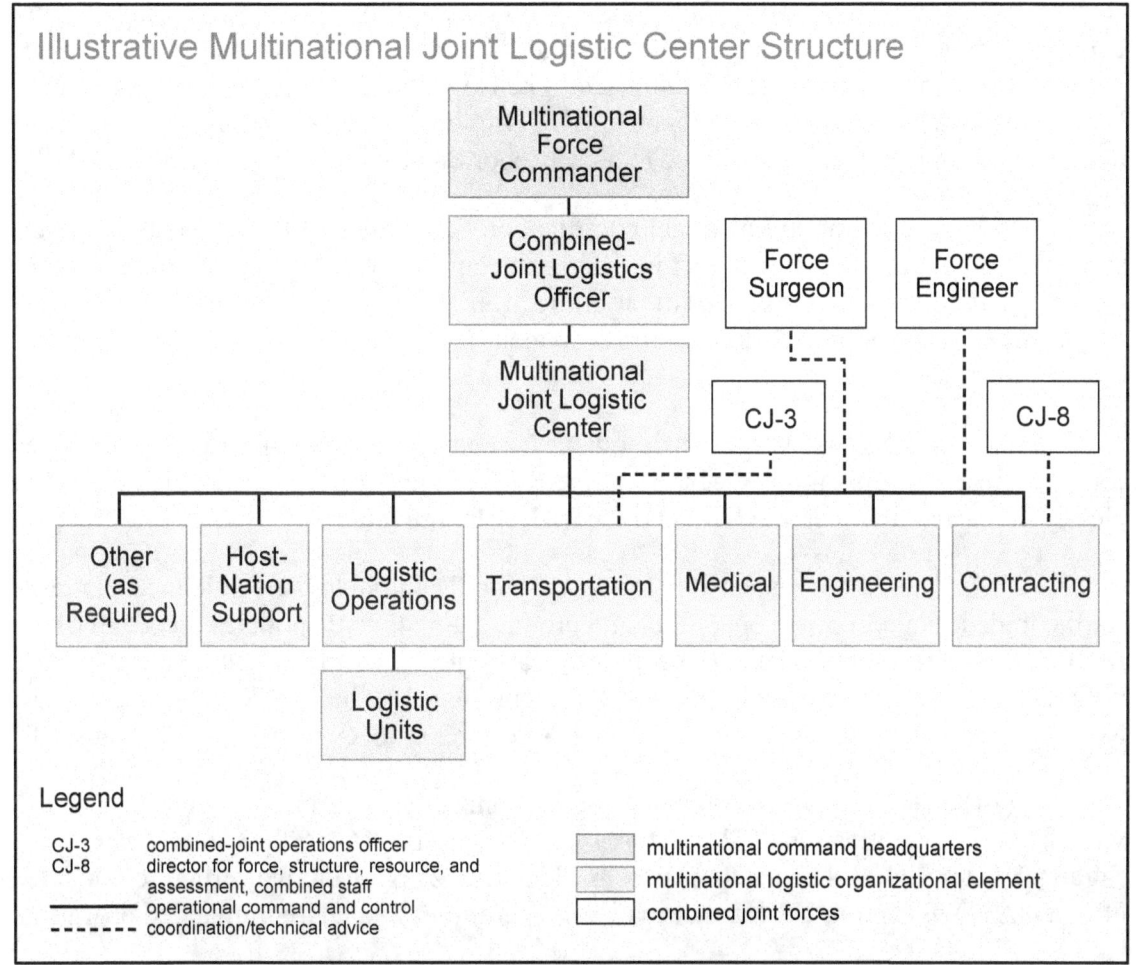

Figure V-1. Illustrative Multinational Joint Logistic Center Structure

blood program office, joint medical surveillance team, joint materiel priorities and allocation board, and joint transportation board.

See JP 4-0, Joint Logistics, *for details on the functions of these centers, offices, and boards.*

(8) NATO has developed detailed doctrine regarding the structure of an MJLC, including the functions and staffing of various coordinating centers. The specific names and functions of these centers are described in AJP 4.6, *Multinational Joint Logistic Center Doctrine.*

(9) Depending on the command structure of the operation, some functions, such as movement control, engineering (general, combat, and geospatial), and medical support, may not fall under the staff cognizance of the CJ-4. The MNFC may determine that these functions will be organized under other staff sections, such as the combined-joint operations officer, staff engineer, or staff medical officer. Nonetheless, the CJ-4/MJLC will be involved in coordinating various aspects of these functions—for example, contracting for local supplies and services in support of engineer and health support activities.

(10) Another important functional task of the CJ-4/MJLC will be to maintain close coordination on logistic matters with NGOs and IGOs through the MNFC's civil-military coordination center or CMOC, if established. The US and other nations participating in an MNF may establish separate national CMOCs to best execute national civil-military activities and objectives. Nations need to closely coordinate their activities with the MNFC.

(11) In addition to functional coordination tasks, the MJLC may be assigned the responsibility for coordinating the efforts of logistic units provided by nations to serve at the theater/operational-level for support of the entire MNF. NATO doctrine considers that there may also be a need to establish tailored component-level subordinate MNLCs to conduct component-level coordination.

(12) Regardless of the specific logistic C2 and/or management structure developed for a multinational operation, execution of the MNFC's logistic responsibilities should be clearly delineated between the CJ-4 and the MJLC or equivalent.

(13) The CJ-4 is responsible for developing the initial logistic guidance, planning for the logistic support of the operation, and promulgating logistic policies on behalf of the MNFC. The MJLC (or equivalent) is primarily concerned with implementing the guidance, policies, and plans developed by the CJ-4 and approved by the MNFC. Essentially, the MJLC performs the execution role for the CJ-4, serving as an extension of the CJ-4 staff.

(14) Regarding the overall logistic C2 organization, several options exist consistent with the various multinational C2 structures described in JP 3-16, *Multinational Operations*. Figures V-2 through V-4 depict three possible logistic C2 organizational structures modeled after a NATO operation, US-led multinational operations, and UN-commanded operation.

(15) The structure represented in Figure V-2 can apply across the spectrum of multinational operations but is most applicable to larger multinational operations with many participants. The key logistic organizational elements of this model are an MJLC, an MNLC for the maritime component, and NSEs supporting respective national contingents. (Depending on the size and complexity of MNF air and land forces, MNLCs may also be established for the air and land component commands.)

(16) In the operation represented, US contingents assigned to the MNF operate under OPCON of the relevant component commander, as has occurred in NATO Balkan operations. Alternatively, US forces could participate in the operation as a JTF and be supported through a combination of Service-specific logistic organizations and a joint logistic organization responsible for providing CUL to US JTF units.

(17) In the structure depicted in Figure V-3 for a US-led multinational operation, the relevant lead service for CUL support of US forces also provides such support to PNs. An MJLC, directed by the MNFC's CJ-4, coordinates selected logistic activities (e.g., fuel supply and distribution and medical support) with multinational partners through various cells and boards. A JMC is also established. This structure is suited to operations where only a few multinational partners contribute to a predominate-US MNF. The logistic

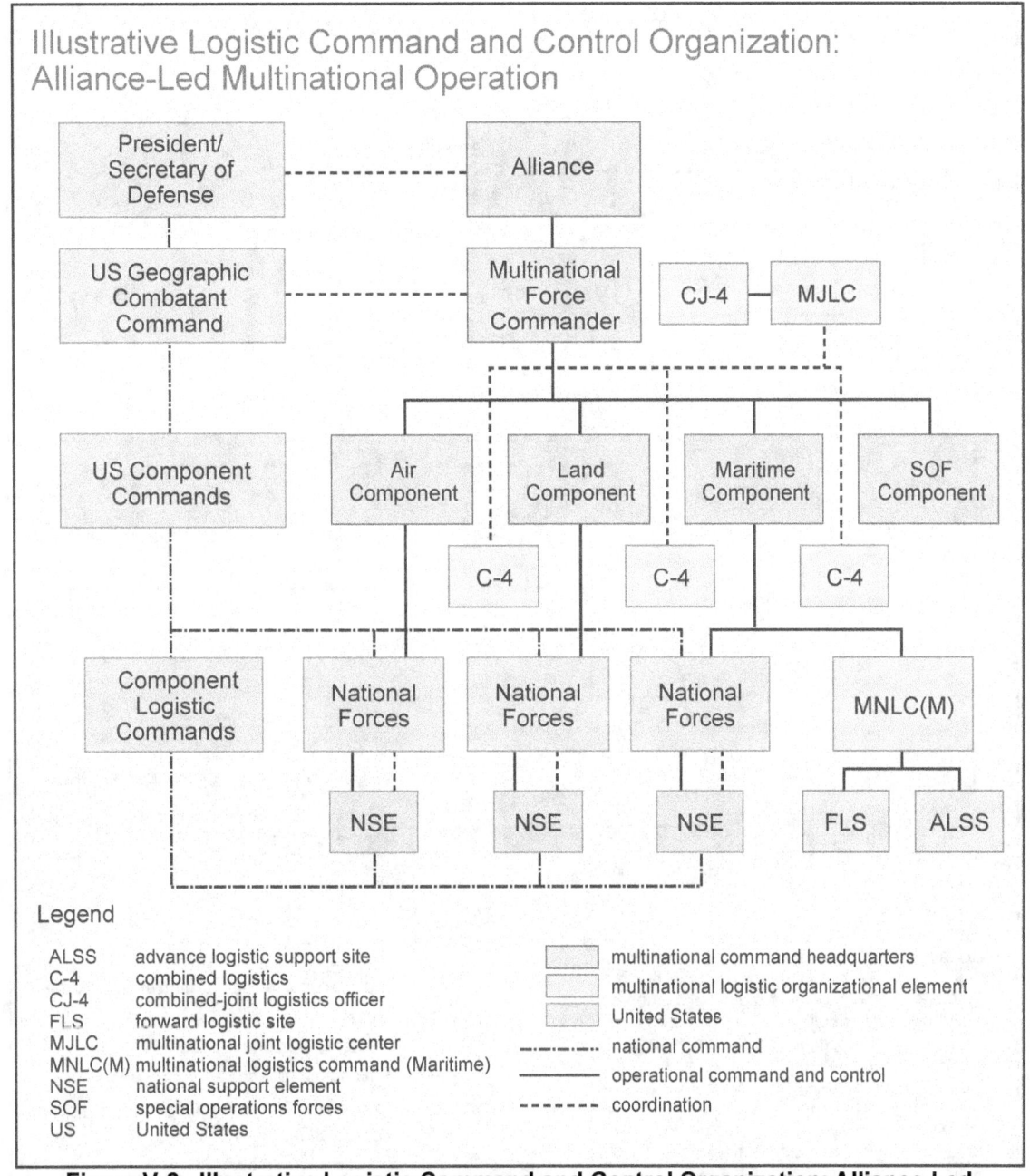

Figure V-2. Illustrative Logistic Command and Control Organization: Alliance-Led Multinational Operation

structure for the operation consists of US staff elements that are augmented with multinational personnel to form an integrated joint structure.

(18) The logistics C2 structure for a non-US-led coalition operation may diverge from the US or alliance models in various aspects. US logistic planners seek to influence the MNL structure of a non-US-led coalition to be consistent with approved US joint doctrine. However, US commanders and logistic staff should be prepared to operate within C2 organizations that differ from those discussed within this publication.

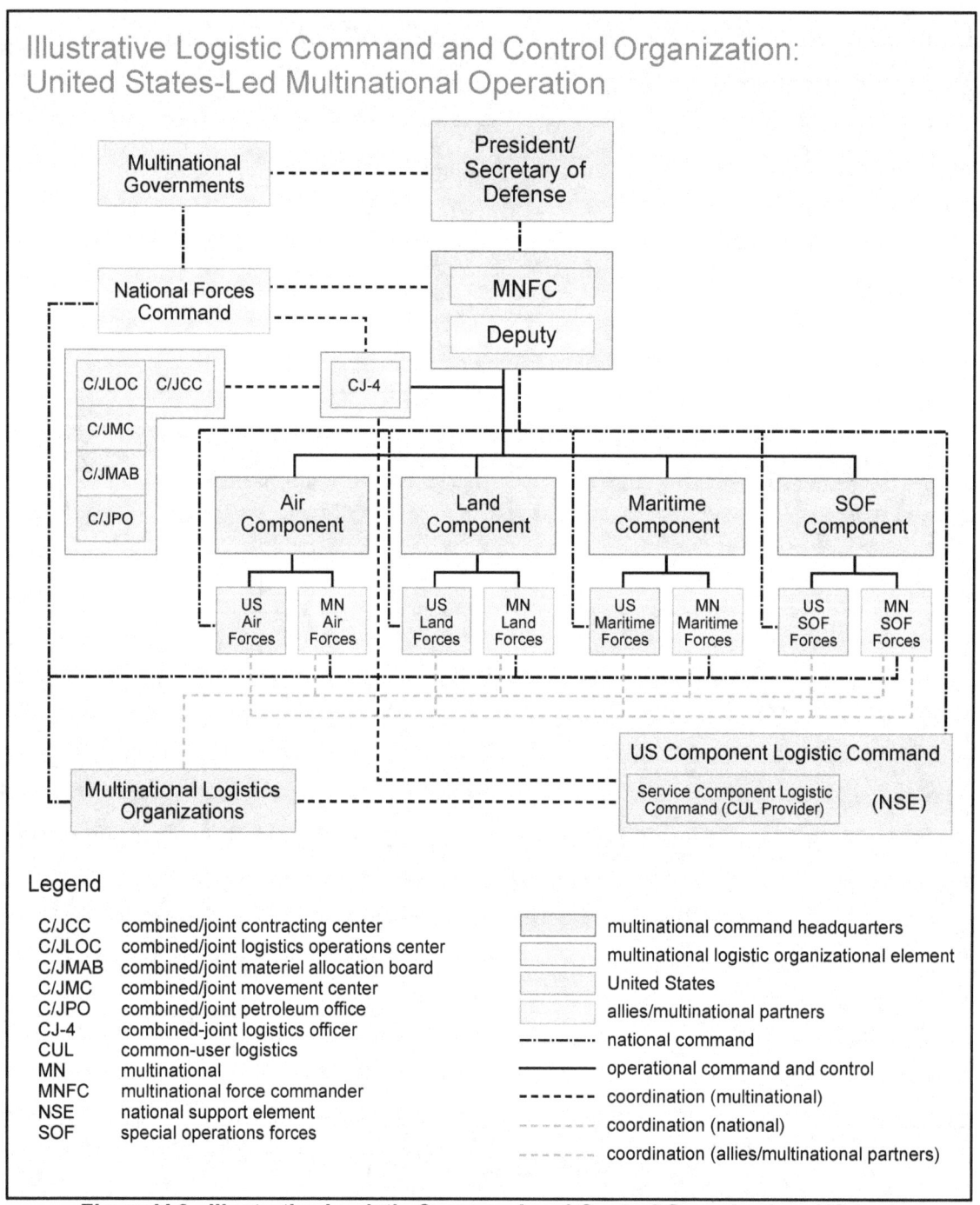

Figure V-3. Illustrative Logistic Command and Control Organization: US-Led Multinational Operation

(19) Figure V-4 represents a key feature of UN operations: responsibility for logistic support may be shared between a force commander and a chief administrative officer (CAO). This dual structure was developed to manage peace support operations involving relatively few military forces (e.g., small peacekeeping contingents and observer teams) that could be most efficiently supported through a single logistic organization. In several larger more recent operations, participating nations have been encouraged to provide their own logistic support for their national contingents. (This support can be provided organically or through bilateral/multilateral arrangements with other participating nations.) Figure V-4 represents such an operation in which the US provides bilateral support to the forces of several other participating nations. Another option is that the US may be requested to serve as LN for the provision of selected logistic support to the entire MNF, as the US did in United Nations Operations in Somalia II. In this case, the CAO exercised overall logistic coordination for the entire UN mission—including the provision of support for other UN activities (such as election monitoring and military observers)—but the US logistic group operated under the control of the force commander.

(20) Other logistic C2 structures are possible. The key is that in multinational operations there will almost always be a requirement for some centralized coordination or management of common logistic support for the MNF. US commands and Services (and their staffs) must be prepared to support US forces in a variety of multinational organizational structures and, in the case of US-led operations, to establish logistic organizations for coordinating logistic support for the entire MNF.

b. **Incorporation of US Theater Management Logistic Considerations in Multinational Operations**

(1) In alliance operations, US forces are guided by previously agreed processes and procedures. For coalition operations, standardization agreements may also have been previously concluded that determine the organization arrangements for an operation. For example, within the ABCA Standardization Program, the participants have agreed to an Army component logistic organization structure for multinational operations that comprise two or more ABCA nations.

(2) In the case of US-led multinational operations, the US JFC is expected to expand upon the tools available for managing joint logistic operations and adapt them to the multinational environment. Current US doctrine for the logistic support of joint operations identifies the need to capitalize on the assets and capabilities available in theater to facilitate support to the warfighter. Joint theater logistics management (JTLM) is one way to help achieve a unified focus within the theater by integrating information, product delivery, flexible response, and effective C2. JTLM ensures that the right product is delivered to the right place at the right time.

See JP 4-0, Joint Logistics, *for additional information.*

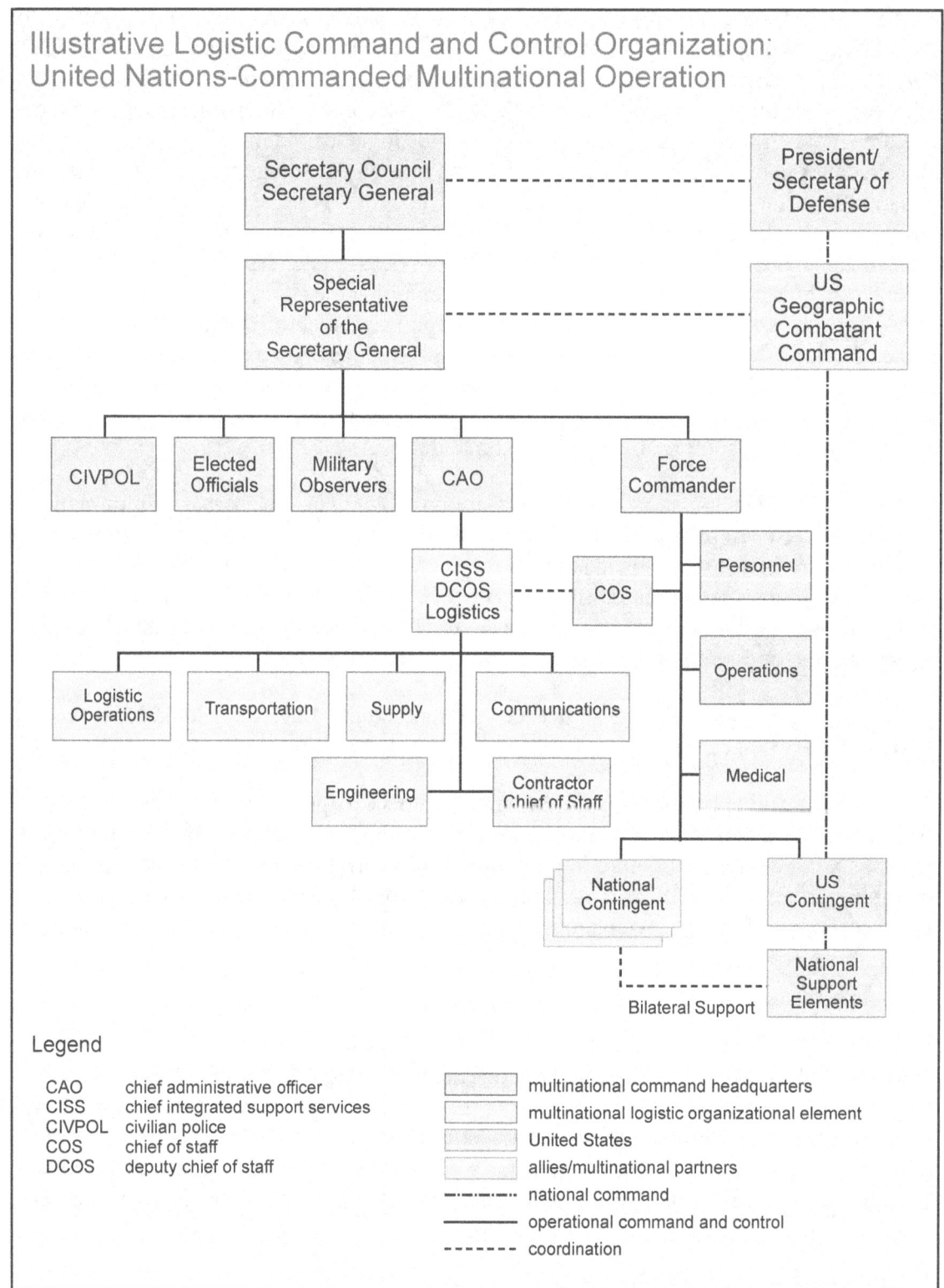

Figure V-4. Illustrative Logistic Command and Control Organization: United Nations-Commanded Multinational Operation

(3) Options for expanding JTLM organizational structures to manage MNL include: using a predominant Service organization as the nucleus operational logistic activity to manage common requirements; expanding the logistic readiness center, and using the lead Service, as directed by the CCDR, to provide CUL support (e.g., fresh water) to multinational partners.

(4) Regardless of the approach, US staff conducting JTLM functions will need to be augmented by personnel from participating nations to give the JTLM organization the capability to manage MNL activities. The nucleus for the organization may be available through US personnel currently staffing logistic readiness centers and/or from other logistic commands not anticipated to participate in the operation as a unit. GCCs can facilitate establishment of multinational JTLM organizations by conducting logistic staff augmentation planning exercises with prospective regional multinational partners.

(5) The challenge for JTLM organizations in multinational operations is to gain visibility of the logistic requirements and status of the total MNF. To the extent feasible, JTLM organizations should strive to use improved communications and modern technology to integrate the logistic reporting and information systems of participating nations. Enhanced logistic connectivity may be difficult to achieve, however, because of the differences in technological sophistication among participants and national requirements for information security.

Intentionally Blank

APPENDIX A
COMMANDER'S CHECKLIST FOR LOGISTICS IN SUPPORT OF MULTINATIONAL OPERATIONS

1. General

Logistic operations as described in this publication cover a wide spectrum of subjects. The checklist provided below offers the MNFC, the US JFC, and logisticians participating in multinational operations a tool for use in planning logistic support.

2. Planning

a. Overall Mission-Force Organization-C2

_____ What is the nature of the operation—its specific mission, the size of the force, national composition, and expected duration?

_____ Under what authority is the operation being conducted? UN? NATO? National governments only?

_____ Will a combined joint task force (CJTF) be formed? What forces will be under OPCON of the CJTF commander or MNFC? How is "OPCON" understood by participating nations?

_____ What is the overall C2 structure of the force?

_____ Will the forces be organized along component or national lines?

_____ Does the OPLAN provide a summary of the requirements, taskings, and concept of multinational operations that logistic planning must support?

b. Overall Logistics Planning

_____ Is the planning for the multinational operation under way concurrently by operation and logistic planners?

_____ Has a JFC been designated to provide US input and interface with the multinational planning element, especially for logistics?

_____ Will the US planning element represent both the operation and logistic communities?

_____ Have the force logistical concepts and requirements been determined and concisely stated?

_____ Have logisticians assessed the feasibility and/or supportability and risks of the mission?

_____ Have logistic policies, processes, and reporting procedures been coordinated, established, and promulgated throughout the force, and with key USG interagency, IGO, or NGO partners as appropriate?

_____ Is a listing available of national doctrinal, policy, and procedural publications appropriate to the level at which the plan is prepared? Are multinational and joint service references included where applicable?

_____ Have logistics-related assumptions been stated and are they realistic?

_____ Has the MNFC identified financial responsibilities of all of the participants and developed reimbursement procedures for CUL support?

_____ Has logistics support been planned for all phases of the operation?

c. **Logistic C2 Relationships and Organization**

_____ What is the logistic C2 organization for the operation? Will an MJLC or equivalent organization be established, or will the CJ-4 (and staff) manage and coordinate MNF logistics? If established, where will the MJLC be located in the C2 structure?

_____ Has the multinational command structure been designed to eliminate unnecessary duplication of logistic functions?

_____ Has the US structure been similarly aligned?

_____ Are the responsibilities for support clearly stated for the following? Are they aligned with the correct authority?

    (1) Supporting command(s)

    (2) Supported command(s)

    (3) HNS

    (4) Other Services

    (5) Multinational partners

    (6) NSE

_____ What directive authority, if any, will the MNFC have over logistic support for the MNF? Will the MNFC have OPCON over any logistic units or resources?

_____ Will the MNFC have "redistribution" authority over national logistic assets, and to what extent has the US accepted such authority? What limits has the US imposed on MNFC redistribution of US logistic assets?

_____ Have coordinating centers been established for movement control, medical support, contracting, civil engineering, and logistic operations?

    (1) Where will they be assigned?

(2) What authority will such centers have?

_____ For non-US-led operations, what (if any) US logistic elements will be attached to multinational HQ?

_____ For US-led operations, what plans exist for incorporating PN staff into US logistic C2 and operational organizations? What arrangements have been made to facilitate integrating PN personnel into US logistic organizations—e.g., introduction to US systems and procedures?

_____ Have logistic supported and supporting command relationships been established or referred to higher HQ for resolution?

_____ Will the US establish an NSE?

_____ Will the mission of the US NSE be to support all US components or will there be separate NSEs for each US component of the MNF?

_____ Will US NSE(s) have any responsibilities for providing support to non-US contingents?

_____ Where will NSE(s) be located?

_____ What US liaison elements are needed?

_____ Does the US have a process to ensure that US liaison elements on multinational command staffs possess requisite authorities and have a full understanding of both US and multinational objectives?

_____ What multinational liaison elements are needed, who will provide them, what qualifications should they have, and where will they go?

d. **Logistic Communications and Information Systems**

_____ Have the communications and intelligence systems been established to rapidly disseminate to all participants, time sensitive logistic related information?

_____ What automated logistic information planning tools are available to support COA analysis and to assist the MNFC logistic staff in ensuring that operational priorities are fully supported? Is a coalition logistic database available to support logistic planning? Are participating nations being encouraged to populate the database with up-to-date information that is usable by coalition logistic planners?

_____ Are national logistic information systems interoperable and workarounds or contingency measures being implemented to facilitate exchange of critical logistic information?

_____ What mechanisms are in place to protect logistic information databases and communications systems to ensure continuous logistic support in case of a cyberspace attack?

_____ Are there sufficient interpreters available for both planning and execution?

e. **MNL Support Arrangements**

_____ What is the concept for using RSN, LN, and MILU arrangements for providing CUL support to the MNF? Have requirements for such arrangements been identified and particular nations, with the requisite capabilities, assigned the relevant responsibilities?

_____ Has the US offered to assume RSN, LN, or MILU responsibilities? For what specific logistic functions and geographic area?

_____ To what extent can the US use external theater support contracting to provide logistic support to MNF contingents? What arrangements (legal and otherwise) need to be implemented to allow for such use of US external support contracting capabilities?

_____ If multinational external theater support contracting programs have been previously established, can such capabilities be used to provide CUL in the planned operation?

_____ Are the logistic capabilities of all participating nations—large and small—being fully leveraged through use of MNL arrangements to ensure the most operationally effective and efficient support of the MNF with the smallest logistics footprint?

_____ Are smaller participating nations who have compatible equipment encouraged to link together to enhance mutual support?

_____ What are the implications of planned MNL arrangements for the size and structure of US logistic forces assigned to the operation and the time-phased deployment of specific units?

_____ Is there a requirement for an MNF-wide mutual support agreement to facilitate mutual support among all participating nations? Is the US able to participate in such an agreement?

_____ What action is being taken to obtain waivers to US legal authorities to engage in mutual logistic support with other nations?

_____ What US element is charged to ensure that the necessary ACSAs and related implementing agreements are in place with participants?

_____ Does the US have an ACSA with each participating nation? If not, what will be the legal mechanism for exchanging logistic support?

_____ What is the opportunity for the US to develop or use existing bilateral and multilateral agreements with PN involved in the operation?

_____ To what extent do participating nations have open foreign military sales (FMS) cases with the US to facilitate participating in US logistic support?

_____ Is the MNFC aware of existing agreements among participating nations in the form of bilateral or multilateral arrangements, funding, and training?

f. **Logistic Capabilities/Certification**

_____ What level of sustainment stocks is mandated by the MNFC to maintain in the operational area? What level should US forces maintain?

_____ Are forces—MNF and US—sufficiently robust "logistically" to respond to increased levels of operational intensity?

_____ Have standards regarding logistic capabilities been established and what organization will inspect and ascertain compliance with logistic-related standards prior to deployment?

_____ Does the MNF logistic staff possess the requisite information regarding participant logistic capabilities in order to properly coordinate MNF logistics? Are there measures the MNF staff can take to assist nations in ameliorating any logistic deficiencies?

_____ Is there a requirement for a formal logistic certification process and, if so, how can it be conducted with maximum cooperation and understanding among participating nations?

g. **Managing Allocation of HNS**

_____ What are the MNF requirements for logistic support provided from sources in the operational area?

_____ What infrastructure and other HN logistic resources are available in the operational area to meet MNF requirements?

_____ What defense articles and services is the HN willing to provide and under what reimbursement conditions, and what resources must be procured through contracts with local providers?

_____ How is HNS provision and allocation to be managed and coordinated? Is the MNFC authorized by nations to negotiate HNS agreements on behalf of nations and to prioritize allocation?

_____ Have the appropriate coordination channels been established with the HN to ensure timely provision of HNS where it is most needed? Have the US and other MNF nations established liaison teams in the MNF HQ and at key HNS locations to coordinate the provision of HNS to national contingents?

_____ What HNS agreements do the US and other MNF nations already have in place with HNs? How are pre-existing bilateral HNS arrangements to be integrated into a total MNF HNS structure?

_____ Have MNF nations agreed on a policy for reconciling conflicts in HNS allocation among nations?

h. **Contracting**

_____ Is the MNFC authorized to coordinate multinational contracting efforts in the operational area in order to ensure that priorities are efficiently supported?

_____ Has the MNF HQ organization that will manage this process been identified?

_____ Are the MNF contracting policies and processes available?

_____ Is a "restricted items list" required to manage contracting for scarce resources in the operational area?

_____ Will the MJLC or equivalent organization be required to negotiate contracts for the entire MNF? If so, have participating nations assigned requisite personnel to the MNF contracting center?

_____ Does the US plan to use external theater contracting during the operation?

_____ Who will manage this process?

_____ Will there be a single MNF manager for external theater support contracting to include HNS, LOGCAP, AFCAP, and other contractor support?

_____ Who will be the US manager to interface into this process?

_____ Has the US identified the main point of contact of contractor personnel, including both theater and external theater support contractors?

i. **Common Funding**

_____ Will common funding be available to support multinational common costs and expenditures?

_____ Has it been determined if or to what extent operational-related expenses will be reimbursed from common funding or sources external to national funding by the participating nations?

_____ Has the US identified funding to support operations and/or to provide reimbursement of expenditures from existing budgets?

j. SOFAs/TAs

____ Who is responsible for negotiating a SOFA with the HNs, including transited nations? What is the status of SOFA negotiations?

____ Who is responsible for negotiating the TAs to supplement the SOFA?

____ What logistics-related issues/items need to be addressed in the SOFA and TA(s)? For example, are US and other national contractors properly included as part of the MNF for purposes of SOFA rights and obligations?

____ What US elements are participating in these negotiations?

____ Has the appropriate authority been delegated to the MNFC to negotiate and conclude with multinational partners agreements deemed necessary to conduct the planned operation?

k. Relations with NGOs, IGOs, and Local Populations

____ How will MNF logistic HQ coordinate with NGOs and IGOs? Will a CMOC be established for this purpose? If NATO is participating, will country cluster coordination meetings be held?

____ What MNF logistic organizational element is authorized as the main point of contact with IGOs and NGOs?

____ What efforts have been made to obtain logistics-related information from IGOs and NGOs operating in the area and to take advantage of their knowledge and contacts in the operational area?

____ What efforts have been made to coordinate activities with such organizations to reduce competition for local resources, enhance operational efficiency, and eliminate redundancy in operations?

____ What is the MNF concept for providing logistic support for the restoration of local government and other civil-military activities? What are the MNF and US logistic requirements to support local populations?

____ What is the MNF concept for assisting local governments and populations through acquisition of local goods and services?

l. Engineering

____ What is the MNF concept for general engineering, combat engineering, geospatial support? How will MNF engineering activities be coordinated? Through what organizations?

_____ Have required projects been identified that benefit the entire MNF (e.g., bridge and main supply route construction)?

_____ What resources will be used to execute these projects? Who will provide the resources?

_____ To what extent are HNS and theater contracting resources available for such projects? What governmental, nongovernmental, and international organizations provide engineer logistical support in the operational area? How can MNF leverage or be supplemented by those assets?

m. **Demining**

_____ What is the MNF demining plan? How will demining activities be coordinated? Through what organizations? What resources will be used to execute demining operations? Who will provide the resources?

_____ What are the logistic support requirements for that plan?

_____ Are US forces trained in the restrictions of demining placed on US forces?

n. **HSS**

_____ What is the MNF concept for medical support? What level of capability are nations required to provide their forces in the operational area? What medical policy and guidance has been issued to participating nations?

_____ What organizational element will coordinate medical support for the MNF during the operation? Have nations identified skilled personnel to staff the multinational medical coordination center?

_____ Are there any existing HSS agreements among participating nations or with the HN? What opportunities exist for multinational arrangements to consolidate and rationalize medical support in the operational area? Have LN and RSN health service responsibilities been assigned to nations? Is there a role for multinational integrated medical units?

_____ What medical materiel (supplies and equipment) can the US offer to provide MNF contingents? Has the US JFC notified the MNF chief medical officer of all US legal restrictions that pertain to providing medical support to other nations' personnel and the terms and conditions of such support?

_____ What restrictions apply to US acceptance of medical support from other countries?

_____ What is the quality of the medical capability in the operational area?

_____ To what extent does US intend to contribute to and use an MNF blood bank?

_____ Is there any plan for the US forces to develop an initial preplanned supply support package?

_____ What are the approved commercial sources of medical products?

_____ Are medical treatment facilities identified to support the operation? What is the status of medical evacuation (MEDEVAC) (intratheater) and aeromedical (intratheater and intertheater) evacuation plans?

_____ To what extent will US strategic medical evacuation (aeromedical and MEDEVAC) (air and ground) capabilities be required to support the MNF?

_____ What is the MNF and US theater (aeromedical and MEDEVAC) (air and ground) policy?

_____ What is the process of reimbursement between US and multinational partners regarding the provision and receipt of medical assistance, including (aeromedical and MEDEVAC) (air and ground)?

_____ Have necessary provisions been made to allow rendering of such health support to foreign forces?

o. **CBRN Threats**

_____ Are CBRN threats known and are US and MNF medical facilities prepared to cope with them (including prophylaxis and pretreatment)?

_____ What diseases exist in country?

_____ What plans do the US and the MNF have to decontaminate personnel and materiel and provide contamination mitigation and consequence management support?

_____ To what extent will the MNF and the US need to provide such support to local civilian population?

_____ Will multinational laboratory support provide for the identification and confirmation of biological and chemical warfare agents and support selected biomonitoring requirements?

_____ Are alternate sites and capabilities identified in the event that key logistics nodes and infrastructure are subjected to CBRN hazards?

_____ Are essential contractors and key civilian workers included in CBRN FP planning?

p. **Mortuary Affairs**

_____ Are mortuary affairs and mortuary procedures in place to service multinational casualties to include recognition of culture differences in dealing with casualties?

q. **Detainee Management**

____ What is the MNF plan to handle and care for detainees? What are the US plan, role, and responsibilities?

____ What will be detainee turn-over procedures and to what nation?

r. **FP**

____ What guidance has the MNFC issued regarding FP?

____ What arrangements have been made with HNs and PNs for FP, especially in rear areas?

____ What FP, if any, will be provided by HN and/or multinational partners to US forces, and what FP will the US be required to provide other national contingents of the MNF?

____ Will there be a lead rear area security coordinator? What are the responsibilities of logistic units to provide local security and to coordinate with the lead rear area security organization?

____ What element is responsible for FP planning?

____ What element will be responsible to identify FP threats?

____ Has munitions site planning been conducted?

____ Have munitions control/security procedures been established?

s. **Environmental Hazardous Waste**

____ Has the staff legal office been consulted regarding applicable HN and other environmental law?

____ What is the higher authority guidance regarding environmental law and policy issues?

____ What legal restrictions apply, if any, including the restrictions on the use of appropriated funds or the requirement to notify the CJCS, the Office of the Secretary Defense, or Congress?

____ What, if any, MNFC guidance should be promulgated?

____ Has an environmental checklist been prepared for use by contingents in assuming responsibility for intratheater facilities?

____ What are the applicable HN and other laws and policies relative to the handling, movement, storage, and disposal of hazardous material?

3. Deployment

_____ What automated system will be used to establish and execute the TPFDD?

_____ What will be the US contribution to strategic lift of forces other than US?

_____ Has the deployment plan deconflicted NGO/IGO and contractor transportation requirements in order to avoid competition for limited transportation infrastructure?

_____ What LOCs are to be established?

_____ What will be the responsibilities assigned relative the LOCs from reception to intratheater destinations?

_____ What en route support will national elements require?

_____ What role will the multinational HQ play with regard to contributing nations and en route support?

_____ What is the MNF requirements determination process for flowing the forces into the theater?

_____ Has an MNF TPFDD/TPFDL been established? What is the method of insertion of forces into the theater?

_____ Is there a need for a logistics over-the-shore operation? If so, is that identified in a separate plan?

_____ What is the MNF plan to manage the flow of force into the operational area for the MNFC?

_____ What will be the US management and operational responsibilities to support deployment?

_____ What is the MNF plan to use US strategic lift capability to support deployment?

_____ What will be the reception ports of entry (to include border crossing points) into the operational area?

_____ What are MNF security arrangements for the POEs/PODs?

_____ What LOCs will be used?

_____ What is the plan to manage use of the LOCs?

_____ What LOC will the US use?

_____ What will be the US responsibilities for that LOC?

_____ What is MNF reception, staging, and onward movement plan to include en route support for US forces?

_____ Has the MNFC selected and allocated staging areas and tactical unit assembly areas?

_____ What staging areas and tactical assembly areas have been allocated by the MNFC for US use?

_____ What MNF agreements have been made for en route support of deploying forces to include the US?

_____ Is the MNFC obtaining clearances for MNF elements transiting en route nations?

_____ What is the MNF security plan for reception points in objective area?

_____ What is the MNF plan for coordinating IGO and NGO movement into the operational area?

_____ What is the process to manage road and rail movement into and out of the theater?

_____ Who has that management responsibility?

_____ Who will be the US manager of that flow?

_____ What are the reception requirements for the force moving by these modes?

_____ Who has highway regulation and control responsibility?

_____ Have custom and border clearances been planned for? Obtained? By whom?

_____ What HNS will be available, if any, to support US forces deploying into the operational area?

_____ What MNF and US logistic capabilities need to be deployed very early?

_____ What initial assets has the MNFC identified as requiring visibility during deployment?

_____ Does the US agree to provide such visibility to MNFC? To what extent will this information be shared with other MNF participants?

_____ What is the mechanism and frequency of reporting such information?

_____ Is there an FP plan covering force deployment?

4. Termination/Redeployment

The checklist for deployment also applies in large measure to the redeployment process. The following represent some additional issues associated with termination and redeployment.

_____ Has the end state, exit strategy, and redeployment plan been developed by the MNFC?

_____ What is the status of the US redeployment plan?

_____ Have the redeployment TPFDD and TPFDL been developed and validated?

_____ What are the HN and US customs/agriculture requirements?

_____ Have the US Customs and Border Clearance agencies, particularly the US Department of Agriculture, been contacted to determine requirements for returning cargo and passengers?

_____ If articles are left in theater, what are the procedures for transferring or disposing of those articles?

_____ What US forces, equipment, and materiel will remain in theater?

_____ What are the support requirements for this force?

_____ What MNF forces and materiel will remain in place?

_____ What is the MNF plan to dispose of excess or unusable or equipment where transportation costs exceed new purchase costs?

_____ What is the MNF plan for disposal of hazardous items?

_____ What is the MNF FP plan for withdrawing forces?

_____ What logistic support will be required for withdrawal?

_____ What is the MNF close-out plan for facilities? Does it include a checklist for environmental issues?

_____ What will be the role of LOGCAP, AFCAP, and NAVFAC contingency construction and service contracts during US withdrawal?

_____ What is the estimated cost for facility restoration?

_____ Who will pay for the restoration? US or common funding?

_____ What is the plan to dispose of equipment procured through MNF resources?

_____ What is the destination for US equipment?

_____ What are the equipment readiness standards to be met before being redeployed?

_____ Where will withdrawing equipment be brought to standards? Are facilities adequate for the task?

_____ Have standards been established for equipment being relocated?

_____ Are there applicable accounting procedures for reporting financial expenditures and have reimbursement procedures been initiated?

5. Transition Considerations

_____ Is a transitional plan available to facilitate deployment and operational assumption of in-place contracts, equipment, facilities, and personnel belonging to another agency or alliance?

_____ Will the US be asked to provide additional logistic resources or units to support the operation?

_____ To what extent can other participating nations provide logistic resources that will reduce the US logistic contribution to the operation?

_____ To what extent have the additional logistic requirements of the operation been rationalized given the increased scope of the operation?

_____ To what extent has the logistic structure been identified to meet logistic requirements above the maneuver unit level, e.g., corps or theater-level logistic units.

_____ How will the US JTF C2 structure be affected? Will the US assume command of the operation?

_____ If the US is to lead the operation, to what extent will its C2 organization be augmented by personnel from other participating nations?

_____ Will an MNFC be established to coordinate logistic support for the operation?

_____ What degree of authority for logistics will be given for the operation?

_____ How will costs of the operation be apportioned among participating members?

_____ To what degree will up-front common funding be made available and for what uses?

_____ Is there a need to develop memorandums of agreement (MOAs) to formalize relations among the participating nations? Is there authority to negotiate and conclude such agreements? Have appropriate MOAs been developed?

_____ What modifications are necessary to existing SOFAs and TAs to accommodate forces from the additional countries? Is there authority to negotiate and conclude such agreements?

_____ What agreements are necessary to permit the redistribution of logistic resources during emergency conditions? Is there authority to negotiate and conclude such agreements? Have all participating nations agreed to those provisions?

_____ To what extent will US logistic policies and procedures be changed to satisfy either UN or regional alliance policies and procedures?

_____ Have logistic policies, procedures, processes, and reporting requirements been identified and promulgated?

_____ Has the ability of transferred units to support themselves and/or logistic deficiencies been identified?

_____ If a NATO operation, to what extent and in what areas will NATO STANAGs be used?

_____ Will the participating nations provide logistically robust units that are self-sufficient?

_____ To what extent can existing contracts supporting US forces be amended to support the additional forces?

Intentionally Blank

APPENDIX B
ALTERNATIVE FORMATS FOR LOGISTICS ANNEX TO MULTINATIONAL OPERATION PLAN

This appendix comprises two examples of formats for the logistics annex to a multinational OPLAN. The first example represents the format specified in Chairman of the Joint Chiefs of Staff Manual 3122.01A, *Joint Operation Planning and Execution System Volume 1, Planning Policies and Procedures*, which would apply to a US-led multinational operation. The second example represents a notional format for a logistics annex for a NATO or other non-US-led multinational operation. The notional multinational format is provided to acquaint US logistic planners with an alternate format that they may encounter while planning to participate in possible non-US-led multinational operations. Logistics planning information applicable only to US forces participating in a multinational operation would be contained in the logistics annex to a separate US-only OPLAN.

EXAMPLE (1): LOGISTICS ANNEX (ANNEX D) TO OPLAN FOR US-LED MULTINATIONAL OPERATION

REFERENCES

1. SITUATION

    a. Enemy. See separate Intelligence OPLAN annex (Annex B).

    b. Friendly. Lists multinational partners and the specific tasks assigned to each, as well as NGOs not subordinate to the operation's command.

    c. Assumptions. Statement of valid and necessary assumptions.

    d. Resource Availability. Identification of significant competing demands for logistic resources at the strategic and operational level where expected requirements may exceed resources. Describes recommended solutions within resources available for planning, including use of reasonably assured HNS.

    e. Planning Factors. Statement of approved multinational planning factors.

2. MISSION

    Statement of the essential tasks to be accomplished as it relates to the overall MNF mission.

3. EXECUTION

    a. Concept of Logistic Support. Statement of the overall concept of logistic support, limited to overarching logistics guidance and intent. This can include delineation of logistics C2, to include use of centralized coordination/management activities and establishment/coordination with NSEs; MNFC's general logistic authorities, including use of coordinating and redistribution authority; delineation of national and multinational support;

guidance on logistic forces in the operational area; reliance on HNS and theater/external theater contracting support; delineation and focus of effort by phase, etc.

b. Tasks

(1) Statement of logistic support responsibilities of the MNFC and participating nations and support required from other US/national/multinational commands.

(2) Assigned support responsibilities of joint/combined centers, offices, and boards, such as those for transportation and procurement of CUL supplies, and others providing services to the MNF (reference JP 4-0, *Joint Logistics*).

c. Force Protection. Statement of MNF FP policy and responsibilities regarding logistic activities in the operational area. Refer to overall operation policy and guidance in separate OPLAN annex.

4. ADMINISTRATION AND SUPPORT

a. Logistics. Includes discussion of specific support concepts for various classes of supply and services that delineates policy, requirements, tasks, priorities, and responsibilities of nations and the MNF by phase of operation and use of MNL support arrangements, such as RSN, LN, and MILUs.

(1) Supply and Distribution. Includes summary discussion of supply and distribution policies and arrangements, including relevant multinational considerations (e.g., use of MNL arrangements and any conditions relevant to the provision of CUL). Detailed discussion and lists of supply depots, terminals, and LOCs are included in appendixes or tabs.

(a) Distribution and Allocation

1. Main and alternate supply depots or points and supporting terminals to be used or considered.

2. Pre-positioned logistic resource allocation.

3. Existing terminals and LOCs, and the known or estimated throughput capability. Indicate the time-phased expansion necessary to support the plan.

(b) Level of Supply

1. Time-phased operating stockage objectives for the operating and safety levels required to support the plan. Stockage objectives reflect the maximum quantities of materiel to be maintained on hand to sustain current operations, which will consist of the sum of stocks represented by the operating level and the safety level.

2. Pre-positioned war reserve materiel requirements to support the time-phased deployments pending resupply.

<u>3</u>. Significant special arrangements, including multinational mutual support arrangements, required for materiel support beyond normal supply procedures.

<u>4</u>. Shortfalls/overages resulting from comparison of requirements and assets estimated to be available (from logistic reports submitted by participating nations).

<u>5</u>. Specify when resupply for materiel support is scheduled to begin and describe MNFC guidance/procedures for establishing resupply.

(c) Salvage. Instructions for, and logistic impact of, the collection, classification, and disposition of salvage. Identifies possible use of RSN/LN arrangements for salvage operations.

(d) Captured Enemy Materiel. Instructions for the collection, classification, and disposition of enemy materiel.

(e) Local Acquisition of Supplies and Services. (US activities are governed by Federal Acquisition Regulations, JP 4-0, *Joint Logistics,* and DOD Instruction 3020.41, *Operational Contract Support.*)

<u>1</u>. Identify acquisition of goods and services in the following categories:

<u>a</u>. The general categories of materiel and services that are available and contemplated as a supplement to regular sources.

<u>b</u>. Those that may be used as emergency acquisition.

<u>2</u>. Assessment of the dependability of the local acquisition or labor source in each of the above categories and the joint/combined element that will obtain or manage the resources.

<u>3</u>. Contracted CUL services (existing or new) that are required to support plan execution and identify the existence of contingency plans to ensure the continuation of these services.

<u>4</u>. "Restricted" supplies and services, if any, whose contracted acquisition by participating units must be coordinated with the MNF HQ.

<u>5</u>. Multinational agreements or contracting vehicles (e.g., MNFC negotiated BOAs) as well as relevant national authorities (e.g., ACSAs) that provide for the acquisition and transfer of logistic support, supplies, and services, between the MNF and governments of eligible countries.

(f) Petroleum, Oils, and Lubricants. Specify any multinational arrangements (e.g., use of RSN arrangements) for provision of CUL POL. Refer to JP 4-03, *Joint Bulk Petroleum and Water Doctrine*, and more specific discussion in separate appendix.

(g) Inter-Service Logistic Support. (In a combined/multinational OPLAN this paragraph will be limited to discussion of any multinational inter-Service support arrangements, e.g., offshore provision of bulk POL by multinational naval forces to army forces.)

(h) Mortuary Affairs. Although mortuary affairs are usually a national responsibility, the US may undertake such responsibilities for other countries. Refer to separate appendix on Mortuary Affairs, or, if not used, indicate the mortuary affairs activities applicable to the plan and policy for providing these affairs. Address cultural issues applicable to the composition of the MNF.

(i) Nonnuclear Ammunition. Discuss any pertinent points, including multinational arrangements, and refer to separate appendix, if necessary.

(2) Maintenance and Modification. Discuss any pertinent points, including any MNFC guidance and possible use of multinational arrangements.

(3) Health Service Support. Reference JP 4-02, *Health Service Support,* and separate OPLAN annex (Annex Q), includes conventions for treatment of sick, injured, or wounded personnel, prisoners of war, and civilians. Discusses support requirements for medical logistics to include blood management, combat and operational stress control, preventive medicine, dental services, and veterinary service.

(a) Patient Movement. Describes intertheater and intratheater evacuation policy and procedures for obtaining both from theater assets.

(b) Joint Medical Capabilities and Casualty Management. Defines five overarching medical capabilities for HSS and capabilities of four roles of multinational medical care available in theater.

(4) Mobility and Transportation. See JP 4-01, *The Defense Transportation System.*

(a) General. Provides general planning guidance to nations participating in the MNF to assist in their planning functions.

(b) Mobility Support Force and Transportation Feasibility Analysis. Provides an estimate of the multinational mobility support and transportation feasibility of the plan (based on nationally developed deployment plans). Discusses items of significance discerned during the feasibility analysis that affect mobility and transportation tasks. Considers the availability of adequate lift resources, airfield reception capabilities, seaport and aerial port terminal capabilities, port throughput capabilities, and other requirements for joint and combined RSOI. Also, assesses any features that will adversely affect movement operations, such as the effect of deployment or employment of forces and materiel on airfield ramp space (to include possible HNS).

(5) Civil Engineering Support Plan. Indicates the engineering support activities applicable to the plans and the policies for providing these services, including reliance on

multinational support arrangements (such as use of engineering MILUs) and use of common funding, if applicable, for acquisition of Class IV materiel.

(6) Sustainability Assessment. Refer to separate appendix that provides guidance on preparing a MNL sustainability assessment for the OPLAN. Completion of such an assessment depends on the willingness of participating nations to provide relevant information on their support requirements and available logistic support capabilities.

(7) Security Assistance. (This paragraph may be omitted from a multinational OPLAN because security assistance is usually a bilateral matter and beyond the MNFC's purview.)

(8) Logistics Automation for Deployment, Force Tracking, and Sustainment General Guidance. States policy and guidance and delineates the conceptual approach for MNL automation support for the MNF. Discusses facilities, networks, and frequency management policies. More detailed discussion may be included in a separate appendix.

(9) Operations Security (OPSEC) Planning Guidance for Logistics. Provides comprehensive guidance for ensuring OPSEC of logistic activities. May indicate restrictions on use of US-only information systems or facilities.

b. Administration. Includes general administrative guidance to support MNF logistic operations (under the MNFC's purview) for the basic plan. Specify requirements for logistic reports, including time, methods and classification of submission. May require a separate appendix describing detailed report formats.

5. COMMAND AND CONTROL

a. Command Relationships. Refer to separate OPLAN annex (Annex J) for command relationships external to logistic units. Describes C2 relationships relating to MNF logistic organizations, including the MJLC and national logistic units placed under OPCON of the MNFC; location and use of logistic liaison officer,; and coordination with NSEs. Designates the component that is responsible for C2 of ports and terminals. C2 of the RSOI mission for specific LOCs must also be delineated.

b. Communications Systems. Refer to separate OPLAN annex (Annex K) for detailed command, control, communications, and computers requirements. Provides a general statement of the scope and type of communications required.

Typical Appendixes to Logistics Annex D will include:

1 — Petroleum, Oils, and Lubricants Supply

2 — Water Supply

3 — Mortuary Affairs

4 — Sustainability Analysis

5 — Mobility and Transportation

6 — Engineering Support Plan

7 — Nonnuclear Ammunition

8 — Logistics Automation

9 — Logistics Reports

EXAMPLE (2): NOTIONAL LOGISTICS ANNEX TO OPLAN FOR NON-US-LED MULTINATIONAL OPERATION

REFERENCES

1. GENERAL

2. SITUATION

a. Friendly Supporting Activities.

b. Resource Availability.

3. ASSUMPTIONS

4. MISSION (or LOGISTIC OBJECTIVES)

5. CONCEPT OF LOGISTIC OPERATIONS

(General Description)

a. General Support Concept.

b. Logistic C2.

c. Logistic Responsibilities of MNFC and Contributing Nations.

d. LOCs.

e. HNS Support Concept.

f. NGO Participation and Coordination.

g. General Concept for Other Key Logistic Functions.

h. Key Logistic Tasks by Phase of Operation.

6. TASKS AND RESPONSIBILITIES (Detailed Description)

    a. Logistic Responsibilities of MNFC and Subordinate Organizational Elements.

    b. Logistic Responsibilities of LNs and RSNs.

    c. Logistic Responsibilities of Contributing Nations and other Troop Commanders.

7. MATERIEL AND SERVICES

(Detailed description of specific support concepts for various classes of supply and services that delineate policy, requirements, tasks, and responsibilities of nations and MNFC by phase of operation, and MNL support arrangements. Those functions that require significant MNFC coordination—e.g., movement control, medical support, civil engineering, and contracting—are discussed in separate sections or appendices.)

    a. General Concept and Responsibilities

        (1) Role of NSEs, Coordination Between NSEs and MNF Organizations.

        (2) Supplies and Services Provided Multinationally.

        (3) Role of Contracting.

        (4) Days of Supply, National Stockage Objectives, Storage and Transshipment.

    b. Supply. (Specific concepts for each class of supply, emphasizing the MNL support aspects, where applicable. List may reflect US 10-class system, NATO's 5-class system, or some other. Types of items included in each category should be clearly indicated.)

        (1) Class I: Rations, Water, Ice

        (2) Class II: General Supplies

        (3) Class III: Fuel and Lubricants

        (4) Class IV: Construction Materials

        (5) Class V: Ammunition

        (6) Class VI: Personal Demand Items

        (7) Class VII: Major End Items

        (8) Class VIII: Medical

            (a) Class VIII-b, Blood and blood products

        (9) Class IX: Spare Parts

(10) Class X: Nonstandard items, supplies determined by standardization action as not authorized for procurement, to support nonmilitary programs

c. Services

(1) Maintenance

(2) Laundry and Bath

(3) Refuse Collection and Disposal

(4) Toxic Waste Disposal

(5) Mortuary Affairs

(6) Facilities

(7) Morale, Welfare, Recreation

(Functions that require significant MNFC coordination are described in the following notional separate sections.)

8. TRANSPORTATION AND MOVEMENT CONTROL

9. MEDICAL SUPPORT AND EVACUATION

10. CIVIL ENGINEERING

11. CONTRACTING

(Including Restricted Items List considerations.)

12. FUNDING SUPPORT

(Especially emphasizing the availability, use, and accountability of common funding.)

13. HOST-NATION SUPPORT

14. ENVIRONMENT

(Including provisions for the handling and transport of hazardous material and waste.)

15. **ADMINISTRATION AND PERSONNEL**

16. **LOGISTIC REPORTING**

17. **LOGISTIC COMMAND AND CONTROL RELATIONSHIPS**

18. **FORCE PROTECTION**

19. **CONTINGENCY PLANS**

Intentionally Blank

APPENDIX C
RELEVANT LEGAL AUTHORITIES FOR UNITED STATES LOGISTICS IN SUPPORT OF MULTINATIONAL OPERATIONS

1. General

This appendix describes the general features associated with implementing agreements and financial requirements of the key legal authorities for MNL operations. As noted in Chapter III, "Multinational Logistic Planning," **US CCDRs may not enter into MNL support arrangements without specific legal authority and prior negotiation of appropriate agreements.** These legal authorities differ significantly in terms of required conditions, type of permitted support, and implementation procedures.

2. Acquisition and Cross-Servicing Agreement Authority

a. **General Description.** The ACSA authority, Title 10, USC, Sections 2341-2350, originally enacted as the North Atlantic Treaty Organization Mutual Support Act of 1979 (Public Law Number 96-323), was developed to facilitate reciprocal logistic support. The ACSA legislation provides authority for US forces to perform the following two legally distinct, although not entirely separate, functions:

(1) Acquire logistic support, supplies, and services from foreign sources.

(2) Reciprocal exchange of logistic support, supplies, and services with multinational partners through cross-servicing agreements.

b. Among other things, the ACSA authority waives selected provisions of US contracting law and prescribes ordering and reimbursement procedures that are more flexible than those permitted under other authorities, such as the AECA. The type of logistic support, supplies, and services that may be acquired or transferred under the ACSA is broadly defined; it includes food, billeting, transportation (including airlift), POL, clothing, medical and communications services, ammunition, base operations support (and construction incident to base operations support), storage services, use of facilities, training services, spare parts and components, repair and maintenance services, calibration services, and air and sea port services.

c. **Items that may not be acquired or transferred** under ACSA authority include weapon systems (except for temporary use of general purpose vehicles and other items of military equipment not designated as significant military equipment on the United States Munitions List promulgated pursuant to Title 22, USC, Section 2778 (a)(1)), guided missiles; naval mines and torpedoes; nuclear ammunition and included items such as warheads, warhead sections, and projectiles; guidance kits for bombs or other ammunition; and chemical ammunition (other than riot control agents).

d. **Implementation.** Acquisition-only authority does not require the existence of a cross-servicing agreement or an implementing arrangement (IA), but should only be used when no applicable ACSA exists. US MNFCs or other elements of Armed Forces of the

United States supporting the US MNFC obtain approval from the appropriate combatant command. Acquisition-only transactions document the terms and condition of the specific acquisition transaction. Exchanges of logistic support (which include both acquisition and provision of support) require the prior negotiation of a bilateral ACSA and IA in the form of an ACSA between the DOD and the foreign nation's armed forces. The IA will contain specific procedures for the execution of transfers under the ACSA, especially Service-specific or geographic-specific procedures. In consultation with the Secretary of State, DOD has the authority to negotiate ACSAs. For approved countries and organizations, this negotiating authority may be delegated to the CJCS, who may further delegate it to GCCs, who may redelegate the authority to Service component commanders. Countries or international organizations that are not pre-approved as ACSA-eligible require consultation with the Secretary of State and advance congressional notification prior to negotiation of an ACSA. Further, prior to concluding an agreement that has been negotiated, further consultation with the Department of State is necessary. Parties eligible to conclude ACSAs with the US include the governments of NATO countries, NATO subsidiary organizations, the UN organization or any regional organization of which the US is a member, and other nations designated by the Secretary of Defense in consultation with the Secretary of State.

    e. **Financial Requirements.** A key ACSA provision is the range of reimbursement options permitted for logistic exchanges: payment in cash, replacement in kind, or replacement by supplies or services of equal value. Furthermore, the terms of reimbursement may be negotiated by the US and foreign parties on a transaction-by-transaction basis. That is, the providing party (which determines the form of reimbursement) may require cash reimbursement in one exchange transaction but accept replacement in kind or replacement of equal value in another.

For further information, refer to Chairman of the Joint Chiefs of Staff Instruction (CJCSI) 2120.01, Acquisition and Cross-Servicing Agreements.

3. Cooperative Military Airlift Agreements

    a. **General Requirements.** Cooperative military airlift agreements (CMAAs), Title 10, USC, Section 2350c, provides authority for US forces to acquire or exchange airlift support from allied countries and NATO subsidiary bodies for the transportation of personnel and cargo of the military forces on aircraft operated by and for each other's military forces. The Secretary of Defense has delegated to the Commander, USTRANSCOM the authority to negotiate and conclude CMAAs.

    b. **Implementation.** The CMAA itself normally sets forth the terms, conditions, and procedures to be followed by the US and the allied country or NATO subsidiary body involved. Title 10, USC, Section 2350c, however, limits the type of military airlift capacity that may be used to provide transportation during peacetime. Operational, financial, and other detailed procedures may be included in a technical annex or appendix to the CMAA. No additional agreements are required.

    c. **Financial Requirements.** Title 10, USC, Section 2350c states that the rate of reimbursement for transportation shall be the same for each party and not less than the rate charged to military forces of the US. Credits and liabilities may be liquidated as agreed upon between the parties, either by in-kind transportation services or by direct payment. The liquidation must occur on a regular basis, but not less often than once every 12 months. CMAAs may not be used by allied countries to transport defense articles purchased under the AECA at less than the full rate of reimbursement that is equal to the cost of transportation.

4. Arms Export Control Act

a. **General Description**

(1) The AECA of 1976, Title 22, USC, Sections 2751-2756, 2761-2767, 2769, 2770, 2770a-2781, 2785, 2791-2795b, 2796-2796d, 2797-2797c, 2798, 2799-2799d, 2799aa-2799aa-2, was developed primarily to manage and regulate the sales of major weapons systems and associated support and training to foreign countries or IGOs, but it can and has been used as the authority for transfers of logistic support. Among other things, the AECA provides authority for the following:

(a) Sales of defense articles or services from existing DOD stocks.

(b) Sales of defense articles or services from new procurement managed by DOD.

(c) Sale of DOD design or construction services.

(2) Collectively, these government-to-government sales of defense articles or services are known as FMS. **The AECA imposes restrictions on the type of articles and services that can be transferred,** and contains specific provisions regarding purchaser eligibility, third country retransfers, congressional notification/certification, and reporting. However, most of these restrictions apply to sales of high cost, high technology weapons systems; few apply to FMS made in support of US MNL obligations.

b. **Implementation.** All sales under the AECA are documented in formal government-to-government agreements, known as letters of offer and acceptance (LOAs). LOAs are generally initiated, negotiated, and implemented by the materiel and logistic commands of the Military Departments and reviewed and approved by the Defense Security Cooperation Agency; the geographic combatant commands (and their components) have little formal role in these processes. The negotiation of LOAs required to fulfill US MNL responsibilities can be time-consuming, particularly when many nations expect to receive support through FMS at the same time. In some cases this process may take 60 to 90 days.

c. **Financial Requirements.** The AECA requires advance payment in US dollars for all FMS transactions. **For US and multinational commanders, this requirement means that US logistic support authorized in an FMS case cannot be provided until the recipient provides and processes adequate funding to the USG.** The advance payment requirement means that no appropriated US funds are involved in the transfer of support under the AECA. Thus, such transfers would not be affected by any DOD authorization or appropriation act provisions regulating logistic transfers involving the use of appropriated funds, such as those under the ACSA.

5. Foreign Assistance Act

a. **General Description.** The FAA of 1961, Title 22, USC, Sections 2151-2431k, contains a broad range of authorities to provide financial aid or sell/transfer free of charge military goods or services to foreign countries or IGOs. Although less important for MNL operations than the ACSA and AECA, two provisions of the FAA are important: Section 506 (Title 22, USC, Section 2318) drawdowns and Section 607 (Title 22, USC, Section 2357) reimbursable sales. Section 506(a)(1) provides authority to the President, on determining that an unforeseen emergency requiring immediate military assistance to a country or IGO exists, and which cannot be met under the authority of the AECA or any other law, to direct the drawdown of existing DOD articles and services for transfer to a foreign country or IGO. The value of DOD articles and services provided under this authority will be limited in the drawdown determination, and the drawdown equipment or supplies must come from existing stocks; no new procurement is authorized. Additionally, Section 506 authorizes drawdowns from DOD inventory or resources specifically for support of counterdrug, disaster relief, nonproliferation, and migrant and refugee assistance. The second authority, Section 607 of the FAA, allows any USG department (including DOD) to provide commodities and services to friendly foreign nations or IGOs, among others, on an advance-of-funds or reimbursable basis. The agency providing support under Section 607 may also contract with nongovernmental personnel to assist in providing that support.

b. **Implementation.** Section 506 drawdowns will be issued by a Presidential Determination. However, support under Section 607 is usually provided under an agreement (known as a Section 607 agreement) negotiated between the intended foreign recipient of logistic support and the US Department of State. The agreement defines the general terms and conditions for any USG support for an individual country or specific UN mission. A signed 607 agreement expresses the Department of State's policy approval for providing US support to a country or UN mission but does not commit the DOD to honor every UN support request. It does, however, eliminate the requirement for Department of State review of individual support requests. Within the DOD, any Section 607 support that is to be managed through security assistance channels (generally equipment leases and repair parts provided by Military Service materiel commands, such as Army Materiel Command or Air Force Materiel Command) will be implemented through an LOA.

c. **Financial Requirements.** Section 506 does not require reimbursement for the provided equipment, supplies, or services, but it does require the DOD to closely monitor the value of stocks and training drawdown to ensure that the annual cap is not exceeded. The act authorizes supplemental appropriations to reimburse the providing DOD component for drawdowns but such appropriations require separate congressional action. By contrast, Section 607 requires the foreign country or IGO to pay for US support, but imposes no specific deadline for reimbursement. If reimbursement will not be completed within 180 days after the close of the fiscal year in which such services and commodities are delivered, then payment of interest is required at the current rate established pursuant to Section 635(b)(1)(B) of Title 12, USC. Repayment of such principal and interest must not exceed a period of three years from the date of signing of the agreement to provide the service: That funds available for this paragraph in any fiscal year shall not exceed $1,000,000 of the total funds authorized for use in such fiscal year and shall be available only to the extent provided in appropriation acts. Interest shall accrue as of the date of disbursement to the agency or organization providing such services.

6. Federal Property and Administrative Services Act

a. **General Description.** The Federal Property and Administrative Services Act, contained in Subtitle I of Title 40, USC, Sections 701-705, permits any USG agency, including DOD, to transfer foreign excess property (FEP) to foreign countries for foreign currency, substantial benefits, or the discharge of claims. Within DOD, pursuant to Title 40, USC, Section 102, FEP is defined as any DOD property, excluding major naval vessels (defined as battleships, cruisers, aircraft carriers, destroyers, or submarines) and records of the DOD, not required for discharge of DOD responsibilities that is not located in the US, the District of Columbia, Puerto Rico, American Samoa, Guam, the Northern Mariana Islands, the Federated States of Micronesia, the Marshall Islands, Palau, and the US Virgin Islands. Property that may be transferred under this authority includes such logistic items as accommodations, construction materiel, food, and medical equipment that are both excess to DOD requirements and/or costly to remove from a foreign country.

b. **Implementation.** Transfers of logistic items under the Federal Property and Administrative Services Act are implemented by a memorandum of understanding (MOU) developed by the cognizant Military Department and coordinated with the Office of the Secretary of Defense. Among other things, the MOU identifies the items to be transferred, the fair market value of the items, and the tangible non-monetary benefits to be received by the USG in exchange for the FEP. **The GCCs have little formal role in this process.**

c. **Financial Requirements.** The Federal Property and Administrative Services Act and the implementing DOD regulations allow the Military Departments and DLA a broad degree of latitude in determining the financial terms of the transfer. DOD requires that transfers of FEP for "substantial benefits" must be in the overall interests of the US and be tangible and appreciable in relation to the value of property being transferred.

7. Transportation Preference Laws

a. Title 49, USC, Section 41106, and Fly America Act (Title 49, USC, Section 40118) require that DOD use US air carriers which are members of the Civil Reserve Air Fleet to meet DOD's air transportation needs when such carriers are available. These laws apply even if a foreign carrier is available, more convenient, or less expensive than a US carrier.

b. The Cargo Preference Act of 1904 (Title 10, USC, Section 2631) requires that supplies bought for or owned by DOD entities be transported on US flag vessels when available and the cost is not excessive or otherwise unreasonable.

c. Transportation preference laws may impact a commander's ability to transport DOD goods and DOD personnel on foreign air carriers and foreign flag vessels, even if such transportation is provided by an ally as reimbursement for other logistic support, supplies, and services received from the US under an ACSA transaction. Operational commanders should consult their staff judge advocate or other legal counsel to determine whether the transportation preference laws apply in a particular situation.

Intentionally Blank

APPENDIX D
UNITED STATES CONTRACTING CONSIDERATIONS IN MULTINATIONAL OPERATIONS

1. Principles of Contingency Contracting

a. The MNFC establishes rules, policies, and procedures applicable to contracting activities in the operational area. However, contracting by US forces participating in an MNF is subject to the same laws and regulations that apply to contracting generally, including the requirement for fair and open competition. Therefore, it is important that the rules, policies and procedures developed by the MNFC be consistent with US contracting law and regulations. Appropriate personnel, including contracting officers and staff legal counsel, should assist the MNFC in developing the MNF contracting rules, policies, and procedures. Such rules may, for example, take into consideration guidelines for simplified acquisition and micro-purchases that are not subject to the laws (Title 10, USC, Section 2304) requiring full and open competition. (See Title 41, USC, Section 428a.) Other exceptions to the full and open competition rules applicable to contingency operations include limited source purchases, compelling urgency, based on international agreements, national security, and public interest (can only be invoked by head of the agency).

b. The contracting rules established by the MNFC are designed to ensure that the MNFC's logistic priorities are fully supported. A multinational acquisition and contracting board (MACB) may be established to develop and promulgate procurement policies and priorities on behalf of the MNFC, in conjunction with the theater allied contracting office, if an MJLC is established. The MACB may assist with developing and disseminating the restricted items list.

c. The senior US procurement official will coordinate with the civil-military operations staff officers of both the US JTF and the MNF to ensure that the staff officers understand the total requirements being levied on the HN through contracting and through requests for HNS.

d. To the extent allowed by law, US policy in some operations may be to award contracts to local suppliers in order to support the local economy and contribute to "nation building."

e. US political and military objectives in some operations may be aided by obtaining contract administration services either from the HN or another PN.

2. Execution of Multinational Contracting Operations

a. Contracting operations in multinational operations require a detailed understanding of customer requirements. Because of the diverse and unique needs of the various nations, these requirements will be much more complex than for US joint operations. Knowledge of these requirements will help ensure customer satisfaction and ensure that the basis for reimbursement is accurate and complete.

b. There must be a clear understanding of the standards of performance required of the contractor. Achieving such understanding can be a complex undertaking given the varied cultures and languages that US commanders may encounter. Because of political ramifications, defining clear performance standards is especially relevant when arranging contractor support from an MNF partner or an HN.

c. The senior US procurement official intratheater will coordinate with the MNF MACB and theater allied contracting office (if established) to ensure that the US benefits from any leveraging available from consolidating requirements for multiple nations. Leveraging possibilities may be developed by the theater allied contracting office and the JLCC, or by the contracting officer on the staff of the MNFC. Leveraging probably will be particularly effective in CUL areas, such as fuel procurement and distribution, construction materials, transportation, staging areas, and lodging.

d. A US warranted contracting officer should be attached to the theater allied contracting office or staff element at the MNF HQ to take full advantage of available leveraging possibilities.

e. US contracting law and procedures will be used by US contracting officers during multinational operations. The techniques will include purchasing locally and using BOAs to leverage consolidated requirements and to simplify the procurement process. BOAs are particularly useful when procuring theater-wide supplies and services, such as office supplies, food, vehicle maintenance, and construction materiel.

APPENDIX E
REFERENCES

The development of JP 4-08 is based upon the following primary references:

1. General

    a. Title 10, *United States Code*.

    b. Title 22, *United States Code*.

    c. Title 32, *Code of Federal Regulations*.

    d. Title 40, *United States Code*.

    e. Title 41, *Code of Federal Regulations*.

    f. Title 49, *Code of Federal Regulations*.

    g. Presidential Decision Directive 56, *Managing Complex Contingency Operations*.

2. Department of Defense Publications

    a. DODD 2010.9, *Acquisition and Cross-Servicing Agreements*.

    b. DODD 4151.18, *Maintenance and Military Materiel*.

    c. DODD 4500.09E, *Transportation and Traffic Management*.

    d. DODD 5100.01, *Functions of the Department of Defense and Its Major Components*.

    e. DODD 5132.03, *DOD Policy and Responsibilities Relating to Security Cooperation*.

    f. DODD 5530.3, *International Agreements*.

    g. DODI 2000.12, *DOD Antiterrorism (AT) Program*.

    h. DODI 2000.20, *Cooperative Logistics Supply Support Arrangements*.

    i. DODI 2010.06, *Materiel Interoperability and Standardization with Allies and Coalition Partners*.

    j. DODI 2030.08, *Implementation of Trade Security Controls (TSC) for Transfers of DOD US Munitions List (USML) and Commerce Control List (CCL) Personal Property to Parties Outside DOD Control*.

    k. DODI 3020.41, *Operational Contract Support*.

    l. DODI 4140.01, *DOD Supply Chain Materiel Management Policy*.

3. Chairman of the Joint Chiefs of Staff Publications

a. CJCSI 2120.01A, *Acquisition and Cross-Servicing Agreements.*

b. CJCSI 2700.01D, *International Military Rationalization, Standardization, and Interoperability Between the United States and Its Allies and Other Friendly Nations.*

c. CJCSI 3150.25E, *Joint Lessons Learned Program.*

d. JP 1, *Doctrine for the Armed Forces of the United States.*

e. JP 1-0, *Joint Personnel Support.*

f. JP 1-02, *Department of Defense Dictionary of Military and Associated Terms.*

g. JP 1-06, *Financial Management Support in Joint Operations.*

h. JP 2-03, *Geospatial Intelligence Support to Joint Operations.*

i. JP 3-07.2, *Antiterrorism.*

j. JP 3-07.3, *Peace Operations.*

k. JP 3-08, *Interorganizational Coordination During Joint Operations.*

l. JP 3-10, *Joint Security Operations in Theater.*

m. JP 3-11, *Operations in Chemical, Biological, Radiological, and Nuclear (CBRN) Environments.*

n. JP 3-13, *Information Operations.*

o. JP 3-13.3, *Operations Security.*

p. JP 3-16, *Multinational Operations.*

q. JP 3-17, *Air Mobility Operations.*

r. JP 3-29, *Foreign Humanitarian Assistance.*

s. JP 3-34, *Joint Engineer Operations.*

t. JP 3-35, *Deployment and Redeployment Operations.*

u. JP 3-57, *Civil-Military Operations.*

v. JP 4-0, *Joint Logistics.*

w. JP 4-01, *The Defense Transportation System.*

x. JP 4-01.5, *Joint Terminal Operations*.

y. JP 4-02, *Health Service Support*.

z. JP 4-03, *Joint Bulk Petroleum and Water Doctrine*.

aa. JP 5-0, *Joint Operation Planning*.

4. Other Publications

a. NATO Logistics Handbook.

b. MC 319/2, *NATO Principles and Policies for Logistics*.

c. MC 326/1, *Medical Support Precepts and Guidance for NATO*.

d. MC 334/1, *NATO Principles and Policies for Host Nation Support Planning*.

e. MC 336/1, *The Movement and Transportation Concept for NATO*.

f. AJP-4, *Allied Joint Logistic Doctrine*.

g. AJP-4.4, *Allied Joint Movement and Transportation Doctrine*.

h. AJP-4.5, *Allied Joint Host Nation Support Doctrine and Procedures*.

i. AJP-4.6, *Multinational Joint Logistic Centre Doctrine*.

j. AJP-4.10, *Allied Joint Medical Support Doctrine*.

k. Allied Logistic Publication (ALP) 1 (D), *Procedures for Logistic Support Between NATO Navies and Naval Port Information*.

l. ALP 4.1, *Multinational Maritime Force (MNMF) Logistics*.

m. ALP 4.2, *Land Forces Logistic Doctrine*.

n. ALP 4.3, *Air Forces Logistic Doctrine*.

o. ABCA, *Coalition Operations Handbook*.

p. ABCA, *Coalition Logistics Planning Guide (QSTAG 2020)*.

q. *Success in Peacekeeping, United Nations Mission in Haiti: The Military Perspective; Published by the US Army Peacekeeping Institute. Combined Forces Command, Korea, Logistic Principles and Policies*.

r. Defense Financial Management Regulation, Volume 12, Chapter 23, *Contingency Operations*.

s. National Disclosure Policy-1, *National Policy and Procedures for the Disclosure of Classified Military Information to Foreign Governments and International Organizations.*

t. National Security Decision Manual 119, *Disclosure of Classified United States Military Information to Foreign Governments and International Organizations.*

APPENDIX F
ADMINISTRATIVE INSTRUCTIONS

1. User Comments

Users in the field are highly encouraged to submit comments on this publication to: Joint Staff J-7, Deputy Director, Joint and Coalition Warfighting, Joint and Coalition Warfighting Center, ATTN: Joint Doctrine Support Division, 116 Lake View Parkway, Suffolk, VA 23435-2697. These comments should address content (accuracy, usefulness, consistency, and organization), writing, and appearance.

2. Authorship

The lead agent for this publication is the United States Army. The Joint Staff doctrine sponsor for this publication is the Director for Logistics (J-4).

3. Supersession

This publication supersedes JP 4-08, *Joint Doctrine for Logistic Support of Multinational Operations*, 25 September 2002.

4. Change Recommendations

a. Recommendations for urgent changes to this publication should be submitted:

TO: JOINT STAFF WASHINGTON DC//J7-JEDD//

b. Routine changes should be submitted electronically to the Deputy Director, Joint and Coalition Warfighting, Joint and Coalition Warfighting Center, Joint Doctrine Support Division and info the lead agent and the Director for Joint Force Development, J-7/JEDD.

c. When a Joint Staff directorate submits a proposal to the Chairman of the Joint Chiefs of Staff that would change source document information reflected in this publication, that directorate will include a proposed change to this publication as an enclosure to its proposal. The Military Services and other organizations are requested to notify the Director, J-7, Joint Staff, when changes to source documents reflected in this publication are initiated.

5. Distribution of Publications

Local reproduction is authorized and access to unclassified publications is unrestricted. However, access to and reproduction authorization for classified JPs must be in accordance with DOD Manual 5200.01, Volume 1, *DOD Information Security Program: Overview, Classification, and Declassification,* and DOD Manual 5200.01, Volume 3, *DOD Information Security Program: Protection of Classified Information.*

6. Distribution of Electronic Publications

a. Joint Staff J-7 will not print copies of JPs for distribution. Electronic versions are available on JDEIS at https://jdeis.js.mil (NIPRNET) and http://jdeis.js.smil.mil (SIPRNET), and on the JEL at http://www.dtic.mil/doctrine (NIPRNET).

b. Only approved JPs and joint test publications are releasable outside the combatant commands, Services, and Joint Staff. Release of any classified JP to foreign governments or foreign nationals must be requested through the local embassy (Defense Attaché Office) to DIA, Defense Foreign Liaison/IE-3, 200 MacDill Blvd., Joint Base Anacostia-Bolling, Washington, DC 20340-5100.

c. JEL CD-ROM. Upon request of a joint doctrine development community member, the Joint Staff J-7 will produce and deliver one CD-ROM with current JPs. This JEL CD-ROM will be updated not less than semi-annually and when received can be locally reproduced for use within the combatant commands and Services.

GLOSSARY
PART I—ABBREVIATIONS AND ACRONYMS

ABCA	American, British, Canadian, Australian, and New Zealand
ACSA	acquisition and cross-servicing agreement
ADAMS	Allied Deployment and Movement System
AECA	Arms Export Control Act
AFCAP	Air Force contract augmentation program
AJP	allied joint publication
ALP	allied logistic publication
AMCC	allied movement coordination center
BOA	basic ordering agreement
C2	command and control
CAO	chief administrative officer
CBRN	chemical, biological, radiological, and nuclear
CCDR	combatant commander
CJ-4	combined-joint logistics officer
CJCS	Chairman of the Joint Chiefs of Staff
CJCSI	Chairman of the Joint Chiefs of Staff instruction
CJTF	combined joint task force (NATO)
CMAA	cooperative military airlift agreement
CMOC	civil-military operations center
COA	course of action
COCOM	combatant command (command authority)
CONOPS	concept of operations
CUL	common-user logistics
DDP	detailed deployment plan
DLA	Defense Logistics Agency
DOD	Department of Defense
DODD	Department of Defense directive
ECC	engineer coordination cell
FAA	Foreign Assistance Act
FEP	foreign excess property
FMS	foreign military sales
FP	force protection
GCC	geographic combatant commander
HN	host nation
HNS	host-nation support
HNSCC	host-nation support coordination cell

HQ	headquarters
HSS	health service support
IA	implementing arrangement
IGO	intergovernmental organization
ISA	international standardization agreement
ISB	intermediate staging base
JCMEB	joint civil-military engineering board
JDDE	Joint Deployment and Distribution Enterprise
JFC	joint force commander
JFUB	joint facilities utilization board
JLCC	joint logistics coordination center
JLOC	joint logistics operations center
JMC	joint movement center
JP	joint publication
JTCC	joint transportation coordination center
JTF	joint task force
JTLM	joint theater logistics management
JTMS	joint theater movement staff
LN	lead nation
LOA	letter of offer and acceptance
LOC	line of communications
LOGCAP	logistics civil augmentation program (Army)
MACB	multinational acquisition and contracting board
MC	Military Committee (NATO)
MEDCC	medical coordination cell
MEDEVAC	medical evacuation
MILU	multinational integrated logistic unit
MJLC	multinational joint logistic center
MNF	multinational force
MNFC	multinational force commander
MNL	multinational logistics
MNLC	multinational logistic center
MOA	memorandum of agreement
MOU	memorandum of understanding
NALSS	naval advanced logistic support site
NATO	North Atlantic Treaty Organization
NAVFAC	Naval Facilities Engineering Command
NFLS	naval forward logistic site
NGO	nongovernmental organization
NSE	national support element

OPCON	operational control
OPLAN	operation plan
OPORD	operation order
OPSEC	operations security
PN	partner nation
POD	port of debarkation
POE	port of embarkation
POL	petroleum, oils, and lubricants
RSN	role specialist nation
RSOI	reception, staging, onward movement, and integration
SOFA	status-of-forces agreement
STANAG	standardization agreement (NATO)
TA	technical arrangement
TACON	tactical control
TPFDD	time-phased force and deployment data
TPFDL	time-phased force and deployment list
UN	United Nations
UNPROFOR	United Nations protection force
USC	United States Code
USG	United States Government
USTRANSCOM	United States Transportation Command

PART II—TERMS AND DEFINITIONS

acquisition and cross-servicing agreement. Agreement, negotiated on a bilateral basis with United States allies or coalition partners, that allow United States forces to exchange most common types of support, including food, fuel, transportation, ammunition, and equipment. Also called **ACSA.** (Approved for incorporation into JP 1-02.)

aircraft cross-servicing. None. (Approved for removal from JP 1-02.)

cooperative logistics. None. (Approved for removal from JP 1-02.)

cooperative logistic support arrangements. None. (Approved for removal from JP 1-02.)

critical sustainability item. None. (Approved for removal from JP 1-02.)

cross-servicing. A subset of common-user logistics in which a function is performed by one Military Service in support of another Service and for which reimbursement is required from the Service receiving support. (Approved for incorporation into JP 1-02.)

dominant user concept. None. (Approved for removal from JP 1-02.)

enabling force. None. (Approved for removal from JP 1-02.)

international cooperative logistics. None. (Approved for removal from JP 1-02.)

international logistics. None. (Approved for removal from JP 1-02.)

international logistic support. None. (Approved for removal from JP 1-02.)

letter of offer and acceptance. Standard Department of Defense form on which the United States Government documents its offer to transfer to a foreign government or international organization United States defense articles and services via foreign military sales pursuant to the Arms Export Control Act. Also called **LOA.** (Approved for incorporation into JP 1-02.)

logistic assessment. None. (Approved for removal from JP 1-02.)

logistic estimate of the situation. None. (Approved for removal from JP 1-02.)

logistic sourcing. None. (Approved for removal from JP 1-02.)

multinational integrated logistic support. None. (Approved for removal from JP 1-02.)

multinational integrated logistic unit. An organization resulting when two or more nations agree to provide logistics assets to a multinational logistic force under the operational control of a multinational commander for the logistic support of a multinational force. Also called **MILU.** (Approved for replacement of "multinational integrated logistic support unit" in JP 1-02.)

multinational logistics. Any coordinated logistic activity involving two or more nations supporting a multinational force conducting military operations under the auspices of an alliance or coalition, including those conducted under United Nations mandate. Also called **MNL.** (Approved for incorporation into JP 1-02.)

multinational logistic support arrangement. None. (Approved for removal from JP 1-02.)

nonexpendable supplies and materiel. None. (Approved for removal from JP 1-02.)

nonstandard item. None. (Approved for removal from JP 1-02.)

pipeline. None. (Approved for removal from JP 1-02.)

principal items. None. (Approved for removal from JP 1-02.)

reallocation authority. None. (Approved for removal from JP 1-02.)

rearming. None. (Approved for removal from JP 1-02.)

redistribution. None. (Approved for removal from JP 1-02.)

restricted items list. A document listing those logistic goods and services for which nations must coordinate any contracting activity with a commander's centralized contracting organization. (JP 1-02. SOURCE: JP 4-08)

role specialist nation. A nation that has agreed to assume responsibility for providing a particular class of supply or service for all or part of the multinational force. Also called **RSN.** (JP 1-02. SOURCE: JP 4-08)

stockage objective. The maximum quantities of materiel to be maintained on hand to sustain current operations, which will consist of the sum of stocks represented by the operating level and the safety level. (Approved for incorporation into JP 1-02.)

subscription. None. (Approved for removal from JP 1-02.)

Intentionally Blank

JOINT DOCTRINE PUBLICATIONS HIERARCHY

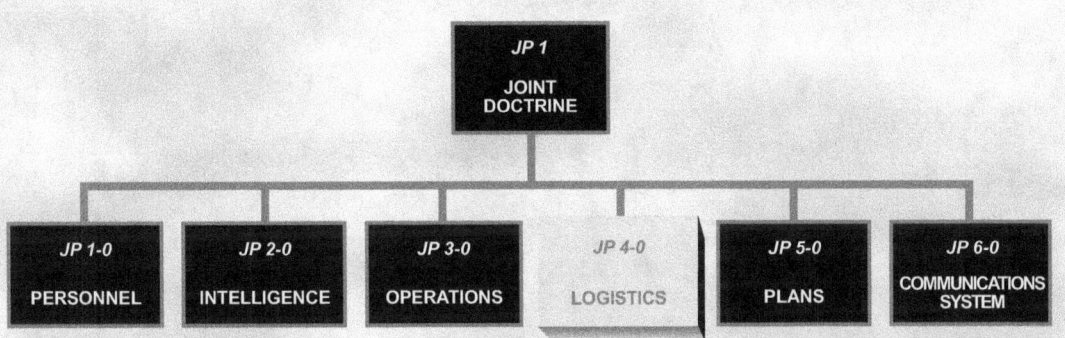

JP 1
JOINT DOCTRINE

| JP 1-0 PERSONNEL | JP 2-0 INTELLIGENCE | JP 3-0 OPERATIONS | JP 4-0 LOGISTICS | JP 5-0 PLANS | JP 6-0 COMMUNICATIONS SYSTEM |

All joint publications are organized into a comprehensive hierarchy as shown in the chart above. **Joint Publication (JP) 4-08** is in the **Logistics** series of joint doctrine publications. The diagram below illustrates an overview of the development process:

STEP #4 - Maintenance

- JP published and continuously assessed by users
- Formal assessment begins 24 27 months following publication
- Revision begins 3.5 years after publication
- Each JP revision is completed no later than 5 years after signature

STEP #1 - Initiation

- Joint doctrine development community (JDDC) submission to fill extant operational void
- Joint Staff (JS) J 7 conducts front end analysis
- Joint Doctrine Planning Conference validation
- Program directive (PD) development and staffing/joint working group
- PD includes scope, references, outline, milestones, and draft authorship
- JS J 7 approves and releases PD to lead agent (LA) (Service, combatant command, JS directorate)

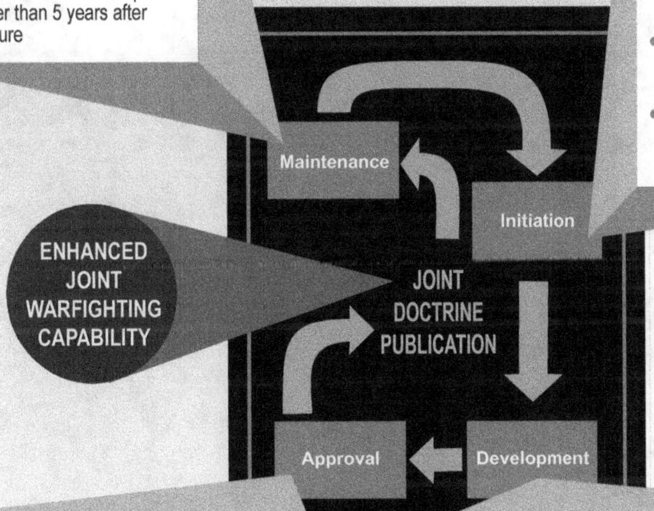

ENHANCED JOINT WARFIGHTING CAPABILITY

Maintenance

Initiation

JOINT DOCTRINE PUBLICATION

Approval

Development

STEP #3 - Approval

- JSDS delivers adjudicated matrix to JS J 7
- JS J 7 prepares publication for signature
- JSDS prepares JS staffing package
- JSDS staffs the publication via JSAP for signature

STEP #2 - Development

- LA selects primary review authority (PRA) to develop the first draft (FD)
- PRA develops FD for staffing with JDDC
- FD comment matrix adjudication
- JS J 7 produces the final coordination (FC) draft, staffs to JDDC and JS via Joint Staff Action Processing (JSAP) system
- Joint Staff doctrine sponsor (JSDS) adjudicates FC comment matrix
- FC joint working group

www.ingramcontent.com/pod-product-compliance
Lightning Source LLC
Chambersburg PA
CBHW081327310526
45789CB00018B/2446